CALAMUS A SERIES OF LETTERS WRITTEN
DURING THE YEARS 1868–1880 BY WALT
WHITMAN TO A YOUNG FRIEND (PETER DOYLE)
EDITED WITH AN INTRODUCTION BY RICHARD
MAURICE BUCKE M.D. ONE OF WHITMAN'S
LITERARY EXECUTORS

"Publish my name and hang up my picture as that of
  the tenderest lover,
The friend, the lover's portrait of whom his friend his
  lover was fondest,
Who was not proud of his songs but of the measureless
  ocean of love within him and freely poured it forth."
              Leaves of Grass (Ed'n 1892), p. 102.

LONDON: G. P. PUTNAM'S SONS BOSTON: SMALL,
MAYNARD & COMPANY. MDCCCXCVIII

811.3 Whi
Whitman, Walt,
1819-1892.
Calamus : a series of
letters written during

WALT WHITMAN AND PETER DOYLE
DRAWN BY H. D. YOUNG FROM A PHO-
TOGRAPH TAKEN BY RICE AT WASH-
INGTON D. C. IN 1869.

ENTERED ACCORDING TO THE ACT OF CONGRESS IN THE YEAR 1897 BY LAURENS MAYNARD, IN THE OFFICE OF THE LIBRARIAN OF CONGRESS AT WASHINGTON.

Written on the fly leaf of a copy of "Specimen Days" sent to Peter Doyle at Washington, June, 1883.

Pete do you remember — (of course you do — I do well) — those great long jovial walks we had at times for years, (1866–'72) out of Washington City — often moonlight nights, 'way to "Good Hope"; or, Sundays, up and down the Potomac shores, one side or the other, sometimes ten miles at a stretch? Or when you work'd on the horsecars, and I waited for you, coming home late together — or resting and chatting at the Market, corner 7th street and the Avenue, and eating those nice musk or watermelons? Or during my tedious sickness and first paralysis ('73) how you used to come to my solitary garret room and make up my bed, and enliven me and chat for an hour or so — or perhaps go out and get the medicines Dr. Drinkard had order'd for me — before you went on duty? . . . . Give my love to dear Mrs. and Mr. Nash, and tell them I have not forgotten them, and never will.

W. W.

WHEN I heard at the close of the day how my name had been
    receiv'd with plaudits in the capitol, still it was not a
    happy night for me that follow'd,
And else when I carous'd, or when my plans were accomplish'd,
    still I was not happy,
But the day when I rose at dawn from the bed of perfect health,
    refresh'd, singing, inhaling the ripe breath of Autumn,
When I saw the full moon in the west grow pale and disappear in
    the morning light,
When I wander'd alone over the beach, and undressing bathed,
    laughing with the cool waters, and saw the sun rise,
And when I thought how my dear friend my lover was on his way
    coming, O then I was happy,
O then each breath tasted sweeter, and all that day my food
    nourish'd me more, and the beautiful day pass'd well,
And the next came with equal joy, and with the next at evening
    came my friend,
And that night when all was still I heard the waters roll slowly
    continually up the shores,
I heard the hissing rustle of the liquid and sands as directed to
    me whispering to congratulate me,
For the one I love most lay sleeping by me under the same cover
    in the cool night,
In the stillness in the Autumn moonbeams his face was inclined
    toward me,
And his arm lay lightly around my breast — and that night I was
    happy.

    Leaves of Grass (Ed'n 1893) pp. 102-103.

I have been privileged to read a series of letters addressed by Whitman to a young man, whom I will call P., and who was tenderly beloved by him. They throw a flood of light upon "Calamus," and are superior to any commentary. It is greatly to be hoped that they may be published. Whitman, it seems, met P. at Washington not long before the year 1869 when the lad was about eighteen years of age. They soon became attached, Whitman's friendship being returned with at least equal warmth by P. The letters breathe a purity and simplicity of affection, a naïveté and reasonableness, which are very remarkable considering the unmistakable intensity of the emotion. Throughout them, Whitman shows the tenderest and wisest care for his young friend's welfare, helps him in material ways, and bestows upon him the best advice, the heartiest encouragement, without betraying any sign of patronage or preaching. Illness soon attacked Walt. He retired to Camden, and P., who was employed as "baggage-master on the freight trains" of a railway, was for long unable to visit him. There is something very wistful in the words addressed from a distance by the aging poet to this "son of responding kisses." I regret that we do not possess P.'s answers. Yet, probably, to most readers, they would not appear highly interesting; for it is clear he was only an artless and uncultured workman.— JOHN ADDINGTON SYMONDS in *Walt Whitman — A Study.* pp 78, 79.

I HEAR it was charged against me that I sought to destroy institutions,
But really I am neither for nor against institutions,
   (What indeed have I in common with them? or what with the destruction of them?)
Only I will establish in the Mannahatta and in every city of these States inland and seaboard,
And in the fields and woods, and above every keel little or large that dents the water,
Without edifices or rules or trustees or any argument,
The institution of the dear love of comrades.

      Leaves of Grass (Ed'n 1891) p. 107

CONTENTS

CHRONOLOGICAL NOTES OF WALT WHITMAN'S LIFE	1
INTRODUCTION BY THE EDITOR, CONTAINING AN INTERVIEW WITH PETER DOYLE	9
LETTERS OF 1868	35
LETTERS OF 1869	53
LETTERS OF 1870	61
LETTERS OF 1871	81
LETTERS OF 1872	87
LETTERS OF 1873	99
LETTERS OF 1874	137
LETTERS OF 1875	159
LETTERS OF 1876–1880	165

I WILL sing the song of companionship,
I will show what alone must finally compact these,
I believe these are to found their own ideal of manly love, indicating it in me,
I will therefore let flame from me the burning fires that were threatening to consume me,
I will lift what has too long kept down those smouldering fires,
I will give them complete abandonment,
I will write the evangel-poem of comrades and of love,
For who but I should understand love with all its sorrow and jo
And who but I should be the poet of comrades?
                                    Leaves of Grass (Ed'n 1892), p. 21

CHRONOLOGICAL NOTES
OF WALT WHITMAN'S LIFE

1819. Born 31st May, in West Hills, Long Island.
1820, '21, '22, and early half of '23. At West Hills.
1823-'24. In Brooklyn, in Front street.
1825-'30. In Cranberry, Johnson, Tillary, and Henry streets. Went to public schools.
1831-'32 Tended in a lawyer's office; then, a doctor's.
1833-'34. In printing offices, learning the trade.
1836-'37. Teaching country schools in Long Island. "Boarded round."
1840-'45. In New York city, printing, etc. Summers in the country. Some farm-work. Writes a number of essays and tales which are published in *Democratic Review* 1841-5.
1846-'47. In Brooklyn, editing daily paper, *The Eagle*.
1848-'49. In New Orleans, on editorial staff of daily paper, *The Crescent*. — "About this time went off on a leisurely journey and working expedition (my brother Jeff with me) through all the Middle States, and down the Ohio and Mississippi Rivers. Lived a while in New Orleans, and worked there. After a time, plodded back northward, up the Mississippi, the Missouri, etc., and around to, and by way of, the great lakes, Michigan, Huron, and

CALAMUS

Erie, to Niagara Falls and Lower Canada finally returning through Central New York, a down the Hudson." — *Personal Notes, W. W.*

1850. Publishing *The Freeman* newspaper in Brooklyn

1851, '52, '53, '54. Carpentering — building houses Brooklyn and selling them.

1855. *First issue of Leaves of Grass. Small quarto, pages, 12 poems. Eight or nine hundred cop printed. (No sale.)*

1856. *Second issue of Leaves of Grass. Small 16m 384 pages, 32 poems — published by Fowler Wells, 308 Broadway, New York. (Little or sale.)*

1860. *Third issue of Leaves of Grass. 456 pages. 12m published by Thayer & Eldridge, 116 Washi ton Street, Boston.*

1862. W. W. leaves Brooklyn and New York perm nently. Goes down to the field of war. Wint partly in Army of the Potomac, camped alo the Rappahannock, Virginia. Begins his min trations to the wounded.

1863–'64. In the field and among the Army hospitals.

1865. At Washington City, as Government clerk, Department of Interior. Is dismissed by H James Harlan for having written an "indec book" — i. e. L. of G. As comment on t governmental action W. D. O'Connor writ *The Good Gray Poet*, adjudged by Henry

2

CHRONOLOGICAL NOTES

Raymond to be the most brilliant monograph in American literature. Whitman at once given another clerkship in office of Attorney General.

1866. Prints *Drum Taps and Sequel to Drum Taps*, poems written during the war, President Lincoln's Funeral Hymn, and other pieces, 96 pages, 12mo. Washington. No publisher's name.

1867. Fourth edition of *Leaves of Grass*. 338 *pages*, 12mo. The poems now begin the order and classification eventually settled upon. New York. No publisher's name.
Notes on Walt Whitman as Poet and Person, by John Burroughs, published.

1868, '69, '70. Employed in Attorney-General's Department, Washington.

1871. Delivers *After all, not to Create only*, (*Song of the Exposition*), at the opening of the American Institute. New York.

1871. Fifth edition of *Leaves of Grass*, 384 *pages, and Passage to India* 120 *pp., both in one volume*, 12mo. Washington, D.C. Includes Drum Taps, Marches now the War is over, etc. (*A handsome edition.*) Second edition of Burroughs "Notes" published.

1872. Delivers *As a Strong Bird on Pinions Free*, at the commencement, Dartmouth College, Hanover, N. H. (now, in 1891 edition, entitled *Thou Mother with thy Equal Brood.*)

CALAMUS

1872. "Took a two months' trip through the New Er[gland] land States, up the Connecticut Valley, Vermo[nt] the Adirondack region and to Burlington, to s[ee] my dear sister Hannah once more, returning h[y] a pleasant day-trip down Lake Champlain — an[d] the next day down the Hudson." — *Person[al] Notes.*

1873. Opening of this year, W. W. prostrated by para[ly]sis, at Washington. Loses his mother by deat[h.] Leaves Washington for good, henceforth lives [in] Camden, New Jersey.

1874-'75. Living in Camden, disabled and ill.

1876. *Sixth or Centennial issue of Leaves of Gra[ss] (printed from the plates of the fifth, 1871, edition[.] Also another volume, Two Rivulets, composed prose and poems alternately. (Very handsome a[nd] valuable. Becoming rare.)*

1877-78. Health and strength now moderately impro[v]ing.

1879. Journeys west to Missouri, Kansas, Colorado, e[tc.]

1880. Journeys to Canada, and summers there at Lond[on] with Dr. and Mrs. Bucke. Made a trip with D[r.] Bucke to Hamilton, Toronto, Kingston, Montre[al,] Quebec, down lakes and St. Lawrence by wat[er] and up the Saguenay.

1881. *Seventh issue of Leaves of Grass, 382 pages, 12m[o.]* James R. Osgood & Co., Boston. Six mont[hs] after issue, J. R. Osgood & Co. are threatened wi[th]

CHRONOLOGICAL NOTES

prosecution by Massachusetts District Attorney Stevens, and abandon the publication.

1882. *Eighth edition of Leaves of Grass, from same plates as 1881 edition with last touches and corrections of the author, containing all the poems from first to last — two hundred and ninety-three — printed under W. W.'s direct supervision. Published by Rees Welch & Co., (afterwards David McKay), 23 South Ninth Street, Philadelphia, also prose writings, autobiography, etc., entitled "Specimen Days and Collect." The author's parentage, early days on Long Island, and young manhood in New York City. Three years' experience in the Secession War, especially the army hospitals. Convalescent notes afterward. Also some literary criticisms, and jaunts west and north. The latter part, Collect, includes Democratic Vistas, the successive Prefaces of Leaves of Grass, with many notes, and prose compositions of various years. 374 pages, 12mo. Published by Rees Welch & Co. (afterwards David McKay.)*

1883. Bucke's *Walt Whitman* is published by David McKay.

1884. Still living in Camden, New Jersey, to which city he came in 1873 and where he remained until his death.

1885-'87. Health steadily though slowly declining — lives very quietly, though many friends (one or

more almost every day) come to see him and in
many ways show an interest in him.
1888. A severe illness (increase of the old paralysis, etc.
brings him to death's door. He never regains
strength after this. *Publishes this year the volume
called, November Boughs — also Complete Poems
and Prose in one large volume.*
1889. The Walt Whitman birthday celebrations were
inaugurated this year by a dinner at Camden (see
the volume *Camden's compliment to Walt Whitman*
edited by Horace L. Traubel and published by
David McKay). *This year is published, in celebration of the seventieth anniversary of the poet's birthday, the limited, autographed, pocket book edition of L. of G. in which is included Sands at Seventy and A Backward Glance O'er Travel'd Roads. (Out of print, rare and valuable.)*
1891. *Goodbye My Fancy published, and immediately afterwards the tenth and final edition of L. of G. including all poems to date.* Of this edition Whitman says that he: "would like it to absolutely supersede all previous ones. Faulty as it is, he decides it as by far his special and entire self-chosen poetic utterance."
1892. *Complete Prose Works, including the previous Specimen Days and Collect published by McKay uniform with above final edition of L. of G.*
Walt Whitman died 26th of March.

CHRONOLOGICAL NOTES

Wm. Clarke publishes *Walt Whitman* (Swan, Sonnenschein & Co., London.)

1893. *Walt Whitman's literary executors publish In Re Walt Whitman.* John Addington Symonds publishes *Walt Whitman, a Study* (J. C. Nimmo, London); also Oscar L. Triggs publishes *Browning and Whitman — a Study in Democracy* (Swan, Sonnenschein & Co., London).

1894. The *Walt Whitman Fellowship (International)* definitely organized on 31st May at Reissers', Philadelphia.

1895. Second annual meeting of *Walt Whitman Fellowship (International)* May 31, at Mercantile Library Hall and Reissers' in Philadelphia.

1896. Third annual meeting of *Walt Whitman Fellowship (International)* at Twentieth Century Club and Hotel Bellevue in Boston (May 31). William Sloane Kennedy publishes *Reminiscences of Walt Whitman* (Alexander Gardner, Paisley, Scotland,) — John Burroughs publishes *Whitman, a Study* (Houghton, Mifflin & Co., Boston) — Thomas Donaldson publishes *Walt Whitman the Man* (Francis P. Harper, New York).

1897. Fourth Annual Meeting of Walt Whitman Fellowship (International) May 31, in Philadelphia. William Norman Guthrie publishes *Walt Whitman the Camden Sage* (The Robert Clarke Co., Cincinnati).

I WILL sound myself and comrades only, I will never again utter a
    call only their call,
I will raise with it immortal reverberations through the States,
I will give an example to lovers to take permanent shape and
    will through the States.

Leaves of Grass (Ed'n 1892), p. 97.

INTRODUCTION

THE broken series of letters (perhaps three lost for each one preserved, but all known to exist included) which make up the body of this little volume, are here given with all their freedom and abandon and literary imperfection *verbatim*. They are possessed of none of the usual merits belonging to the published specimens of this form of composition, and to those who know nothing of the author of *Leaves of Grass* it is very likely they may appear quite valueless. Readers, however, who know something of him will find in them a homely, honest and wholesome flavor very far from displeasing — will detect in them a sweet and nourishing quality comparable to that of the plain food fresh gathered from the pastures, the woods, the fields or the garden. But since in order to derive enjoyment and benefit from them, it is essential that the reader know something of the writer, I have thought well in offering them to the general public to prefix some notes tending to throw light upon the personality of the man, Walt Whitman. And first (avoiding as far as possible repetition of what has elsewhere been written) a few words of my own personal experience.

CALAMUS

I saw him first in 1877, three years before the last of these letters were written. It was one hot July day, the place of meeting, Camden, New Jersey. I had, unasked, a stranger, called to see the man whose own writings (for many years I had read the *Leaves* with delight and enthusiasm) and the writings of others about him had awakened in me profound interest.

The house was a three story red brick, on the street, facing the south. I rang the bell. The door was opened by a pleasant-faced, almost pretty, middle-aged woman, whom I afterwards knew well (and very much liked) as Mrs. George Whitman — the wife of the poet's brother. When I had told her who I had come to see she called up the stairs — "Walt — Walt — here is some one to see you," and showed me into a very comfortable sitting-room to the left of the entrance hall. I had only sat a few minutes in the darkened and comparatively cool room when Walt Whitman entered. He walked slowly leaning on a cane — his left leg, manifestly weaker than the right, making him quite lame. He was suffering from the paralysis mentioned in the letters.

He was a man of about six feet in height and weighing about two hundred pounds, erect, broad chested, dressed in a light gray suit — a white shirt with broad turned-down collar open at the throat and no necktie. His face was broad and red, the picture of robust health, his hair and beard long and almost white. After he had welcomed me, which he did with cordiality, and we had

INTRODUCTION

sat down to talk I saw that his eyes, which were a good part of the time half covered by heavy lids, were pale blue, that his nose was strong and straight, his lips full and more expressive of tenderness than firmness, his cheeks rosy and smooth almost as a boy's — his ears large, fleshy and extraordinarily handsome, his head massive and well rounded both from front to back and from side to side, his brows prominent and very high-arched. His open shirt showed the gray hair of his chest. Head and body were well and somewhat proudly carried. His ruddy face, his flowing, almost white, hair and beard, his spotless linen, his plain, fresh looking gray garments, exhaled an impalpable odor of purity. Almost the dominant initial feeling was: here is a man who is absolutely clean and sweet — and with this came upon me an impression of the man's simple majesty, such as might be produced by an immense handsome tree, or a large, magnificent, beautiful animal.

The poet's voice, which was soft, clear and sympathetic, added much to the charm of his presence. In his speech there was no attempt at smartness or cleverness — the reverse, indeed, of all that. His language was simple, sincere and direct, just as it is in these letters and in all his writings.

After sitting for a time in the room we took the street cars to the Delaware, crossed by the ferry, and then, by an open car, rode several miles up Market Street, Philadelphia. As we passed along I noticed that the men

CALAMUS

and boys, drivers, conductors, ferry hands, laborers, shoe-blacks, news-boys and the rest nearly all seemed to know my companion, and the unmistakable glance of affection which many of them gave in return for his quiet word or nod of recognition was something new in my experience of humanity and so far it has not been paralleled since.

Upon our return to the Delaware we parted, he taking the ferry back to Camden, I returning to my hotel in Philadelphia. Any attempt to convey to another even the faintest notion of the effect upon me of that short and seemingly commonplace interview would be certainly hopeless, probably foolish. Briefly, it would be nothing more than the simple truth to state that I was, by it, lifted to and set upon a higher plane of existence, upon which I have more or less continuously lived ever since — that is, for a period of eighteen years. And my feeling toward the man, Walt Whitman, from that day to the present has been and is that of the deepest affection and reverence. All this, no doubt, was supplemented and reinforced by other meetings, by correspondence and by readings, but equally certainly it derived its initial and essential vitality from that first, almost casual contact.

If it were possible to me I should like, in this brief introduction, to present the man Walt Whitman to the reader as he was at the time these letters were being penned. I have given, in few words, what I saw of him myself at that time. Another and a better observer, John Burroughs, by, for our present purpose, a wonderful

INTRODUCTION

stroke of luck has the following about him.* While ac ually riding on the street car of which Peter Doyle wa conductor, he says: "I give here a glimpse of him i Washington on a Navy Yard horse car, toward th close of the war,† one summer day at sundown. Th car is crowded and suffocatingly hot, with many passer gers on the rear platform, and among them a bearded florid-faced man, elderly, but agile, resting against th dash, by the side of the young conductor, and evidentl his intimate friend. The man wears a broad-brin white hat. Among the jam inside near the door, young Englishwoman, of the working class, with tw children, has had trouble all the way with the youngest a strong, fat, fretful, bright babe of fourteen or fiftee months, who bids fair to worry the mother completel out, besides becoming a howling nuisance to everybody As the car tugs around Capitol Hill the young one i more demoniac than ever, and the flushed and perspir ing mother is just ready to burst into tears with weari ness and vexation. The cars stops at the top of the Hill to let off most of the rear platform passengers, and the white-hatted man reaches inside and gently bu firmly disengaging the babe from its stifling place in the mother's arms, takes it in his own, and out in the air. The astonished and excited child, partly in fear

* *Birds and Poets* — Hurd and Houghton — N. Y. 1877 — pp. 22, et seq.

† An error — it was after the war, probably in 1867.

partly in satisfaction at the change, stops its screaming, and as the man adjusts it more securely to his breast, plants its chubby hands against him, and pushing off as far as it can, gives a good long look squarely in his face — then as if satisfied snuggles down with its head on his neck, and in less than a minute is sound and peacefully asleep without another whimper, utterly fagged out. A square or so more and the conductor, who has had an unusually hard and uninterrupted day's work, gets off for his first meal and relief since morning. And now the white-hatted man, holding the slumbering babe also, acts as conductor the rest of the distance, keeping his eye on the passengers inside, who have by this time thinned out greatly. He makes a very good conductor, too, pulling the bell to stop or go on as needed, and seems to enjoy the occupation. The babe meanwhile rests its fat cheeks close on his neck and gray beard, one of his arms vigilantly surrounding it, while the other signals, from time to time, with the strap; and the flushed mother inside has a good half hour to breathe, and cool, and recover herself." Elsewhere the same writer — then living in Washington and seeing Whitman almost every day, drew from the life the following outline sketch: * "Lethargic during an interview, passive and receptive, an admirable listener, never in a hurry, with the air of one who has plenty of leisure, always in per-

* *Galaxy*, 1 Dec. '66 — pp. 609 et seq.

INTRODUCTION

fect repose, simple and direct in manners, a lover of plain, common people, 'meeter of savage and gentleman on equal terms,' temperate, chaste, sweet-breathed, tender and affectionate, of copious friendship, preferring always to meet as flesh and blood, and with a large, summery, motherly soul that shines in all his ways and looks, he is by no means the 'rough' people have been so willing to believe. Fastidious as a high caste Brahmin in his food and personal neatness and cleanliness, well dressed, with a gray, open throat, a deep sympathetic voice, a kind, genial look, the impression he makes upon you is that of the best blood and breeding. He reminds one of the first men — the beginners; has a primitive out-door look — not so much from being in the open air as from the texture and quality of his make — a look as of the earth, the sea, or the mountains, and 'is usually taken,' says a late champion of his cause, 'for some great mechanic, or stevedore, or seaman, or grand laborer, of one kind or another.' His physiognomy presents very marked features — features of the true antique pattern, almost obsolete in modern faces — seen in the strong, square bridge of his nose, his high arching brows, and the absence of all bulging in his forehead, a face approximating in type to the statued Greek. He does not mean intellect merely, but life: and one feels that he must arrive at his results rather by sympathy and absorption than by hard intellectual processes; by the effluence of power rather than

CALAMUS

by direct and total application of it. In keeping wit
this, his poems do not have the character of carefull
elaborated specimens — of gems cut and polished by th
intellect, but are warm and vascular, like living organism:

"In the matter of health he is an exception to mos
known instances. He presents the rare phenomeno
of a man giving himself to intellectual labor withou
suffering the slightest detriment to his physical powers
never knowing dyspepsia, nervousness, ennui, and a
entire stranger to headache until his presence in th
army hospitals, and his stopping too long consecutivel
after the battles of the Wilderness with a collection o
gangrened wounds, had inoculated his system with
malignant virus. And this robust bodily health, as w
have said, is one key to his poems. The peculiar qualit
of them — a quality as of the open air, the woods, th
shore, we believe to be more or less attributable to thi
source. The absence of all pettiness, dallying and sen
timentalism, follows from a like cause."

I turn now to some words written of him about th
same date by a man well entitled to be heard whereve
Walt Whitman is the subject of discussion. A man wel
worth knowing for his own sake — a man of genius — a1
observer, a thinker, and a powerful writer. A warn
lover of Whitman and of the cause for which Whitmar
lived and worked — William Douglas O'Connor,* speak

* *Three Tales* — Houghton, Mifflin & Co. New York — 1892 —
pp. 239 et seq.

INTRODUCTION

ing of his friend in '67 (just before the earlier of the letters here given were written) says: "He was tall and stalwart: a brow not large, but full, and seamed with kindly wrinkles: a complexion of rosy clearness: heavy-lidded, firm blue eyes, which had a steadfast and draining regard: a short, thick, gray beard almost white, and thinly flowing dark gray hair. His countenance expressed a rude sweetness. He was dressed in a long, dark overcoat, much worn, and of such uncertain fashion that it almost seemed a gaberdine. As he stood there in the gracious darkling light, he looked an image of long and loving experience with men, of immovable composure and charity, of serene wisdom, of immortal rosy youth in reverend age. A faint perfume exhaled from his garments. In the lapel of his coat he wore a sprig of holly. In his aspect were singularly blended the prophet and the child. The child in him inspired love: the prophet, awe. He drew and he repelled.

"In a way quite in keeping with his unconventional aspect and manner he moved with a sort of measured alertness among the group, paying his simple and affectionate addresses to each person, with the air of being already on familiar terms with them, and of knowing all about them: thus establishing himself in close rapport with every one, as only a man with powerful intuitions, vivid impressions, and great magnetic force and dignity could have done, and leaving them with a sense as if something electric and very sweet had swept through them.

  * * * * * *

"He advanced with solemn and stately tread, composed and calm, but dilated to his fullest manly majesty, and from brow to foot he seemed clothed with an august and strong illumination.

  * * * * * *

"In the long soundless pause, it seemed as if heaven and earth were still. * * * *
A change had come upon him. The rosy color had died from his face in a clear splendor, and his form, regnant and masculine, was clothed with inspiration, as with a dazzling aureole. * * *

"'Love' said the gray redeemer, lifting his clear face, bright with deathless smiling, and wet with the sweet waters of immortal tears, 'love, love! That includes all. There is nothing in the world but that — nothing in all the world. Better than all is love. Love is better than all.'"

That the friendship existing between Walt Whitman and Peter Doyle was, as compared with the average sentiment that passes under that name, exceptional and remarkable there can be no doubt, but it does not seem at all clear that there was anything about it which was out of the regular and ordinary course when considered as a fact in the life of Whitman. The present editor possesses a series of letters by the poet to other young men evincing

INTRODUCTION

nearly as great if not as great affection on his part, and that section of the *Leaves* named *Calamus* (written long before he knew Doyle) proves the existence of previous friendships at least equally warm and tender. I give here two letters at random (I could give a small volume of such) for the purpose of illustrating what seems to me Whitman's phenomenal capacity for friendship.

"Oct. 2, '68 — Dear friend Harry Hurt — I thought I would just drop you a line for yourself — but no doubt you keep fully posted about me by my letters to Pete, as I am willing you or any of my particular friends who wish to, should read them (he knows who I would be willing should read them — I leave it to him) — Harry, you would much enjoy going round N. Y. with me, if it were possible, and then how much I should like having you with me. This great city, with all its crowds and splendor, and Broadway fashion and women, and amusements, and the river and bay, and shipping, and the many magnificent new buildings, and Central Park and 5th Avenue, and the endless processions of private vehicles and the finest teams I ever saw, for miles long of a fine afternoon — altogether, they make up a show that I can richly spend a month in enjoying — for a change from my Washington life. I sometimes think that I am the particular man who enjoys the show of all these things in N. Y. more than any other mortal — as if was all got up just for me to observe and study. Harry, I wish when you see Ben. Thompson, conductor, you would say I sent him my

CALAMUS

love and have not forgot him. Let him read this letter. I send him a Newspaper, the N. Y. Clipper. I have marked the piece about the Five Points. I went down there myself for fun, three nights ago, with a friend of mine, a policeman, and that account in the Clipper is a very good description — only not half rank enough. I wish you to tell John Towers, conductor, I send him my love, and we will see each other again one of these days. I send him a Clipper also with an account of the Five Points — Harry, you let one of them lend you the paper, and read the account — it will amuse you — I was there two hours — it was instructive but disgusting — I saw one of the handsomest white girls there I ever saw, only about 18 — black and white are all intermingled."

The other is as follows:

"Oct. '68. Dear Lewy, I will write you just a line to let you know I have not forgotten you. I am here on leave, and shall stay nearly all this month. Duffy is here driving on Broadway and 5th av. line. He has been up the Hudson River this summer driving hotel coach. He is the same old Duffy. I have heard that William Sydnor on 65, was laid up sick. I wish to hear about him, and whether he is well, and again at work. If you see him tell him I have not forgot him, but send him my love and will be back in Washington again. Tell Johnny Miller there is still a sprinkling of the old Broadway drivers left Balky Bill, Fred Kelley, Charley McLaughlin, Tom Riley Prodigal, Sandy, etc., etc., are still here. Frank Mc

INTERVIEW WITH PETER DOYLE

Kinney, and several other old drivers are with Adams Express. Staging is rather dull."

And finally — far more important in this connection than anything that I or any one else could say — I give the result of an interview with the man to whom the letters were addressed.

In May, 1895, in company with Horace L. Traubel, I visited Doyle, whom I had known for years but had not seen for a long time. I explained to him that it was my intention to publish these letters and asked him if he felt there was any insuperable objection? He first inquired — " Of what use are they?" and then, upon my assurance that (in some measure) they would do for the world the same service they had done for him, he further inquired: "Do you think Walt, if he were here, if he could be asked, would be willing?" Whereupon, I, answering affirmatively, was told that I should "go ahead," doing that which seemed to me best, since he felt "entirely safe" in my hands. It was likewise by Doyle's consent that Mr. Traubel took notes of the conversation that ensued, and it is only after his revision that these are printed in this volume. The conversation was desultory but serves to show what manner of man Doyle is and by what sacred ties he feels himself still indissolubly bound to Whitman. Mr. Doyle is reported almost absolutely in his own words. He said : —

I was born in 1847, in Ireland, and was about two

CALAMUS

years old when brought to America. Father was a blacksmith. We lived our first years in America at Alexandria, Virginia. Bad times came on in 1856-7. Father went to Richmond, where he had been offered a place in an iron foundry. While there I was a member of the Fayette Artillery, and when the war broke out I entered the Confederate Army. Getting my parole in Washington, forced to look out for myself, I hung round that region with no particular object in view. I might have been more successful somewhere else, but I was there, and so I just stuck to the case as it was. I became a horse-car conductor. This other business came later on. Yes, I will talk of Walt, nothing suits me better. I will commence anywhere. When you are tired stop me. Walt never used to take much to newspaper men in the old time. There were some few in Washington he rather favored. They always made a good deal of him, of course —that is, they came to him often enough for news or opinions or such stuff. He could shut a man off in the best style, you know. He had a freezing way in him— yet was never harsh. But people got to know that he meant what he said. He said " no " and " no " it was. I remember one special night, we met a half-loaded fellow with some of his journalist friends— a newspaper man, since prominent, who was then pretty well acquanted with Walt. This man was offensively familiar with Walt— insisted on introducing his friends, and all that. Walt held him off —froze him out— would not be introduced.

INTERVIEW WITH PETER DOYLE

It was simply impossible for the intruder to make his point. Now, Walt was always dignified — simple enough, too — and this is a sample of the manner he showed to all alike, famous or plain folks, who stepped across what he thought his private border-line.

How different Walt was then in Washington from the Walt you knew in the later years! You would not believe it. He was an athlete — great, great. I knew him to do wonderful lifting, running, walking. You ask where I first met him? It is a curious story. We felt to each other at once. I was a conductor. The night was very stormy, — he had been over to see Burroughs before he came down to take the car — the storm was awful. Walt had his blanket — it was thrown round his shoulders — he seemed like an old sea-captain. He was the only passenger, it was a lonely night, so I thought I would go in and talk with him. Something in me made me do it and something in him drew me that way. He used to say there was something in me had the same effect on him. Anyway, I went into the car. We were familiar at once — I put my hand on his knee — we understood. He did not get out at the end of the trip — in fact went all the way back with me. I think the year of this was 1866. From that time on we were the biggest sort of friends. I stayed in Washington until 1872, when I went on the Pennsylvania Railroad. Walt was then in the Attorney-General's office. I would frequently go out to the Treasury to see Walt; Hubley Ashton was commonly there — he would be leaning familiarly on the desk where Walt would be writing. They were fast friends — talked a good deal together. Walt rode with me often — often at noon, always at night. He rode round with me on the last trip — sometimes rode for several trips. Everybody knew him. He had a way of taking the measure of the driver's hands — had calf-skin gloves made for them every winter in Georgetown — these gloves were his personal presents to the men. He saluted the men on the other cars as we passed — threw up his hand. They cried to him, " Hullo, Walt! " and he would reply, " Ah, there! " or something like. He was welcome always as the flowers in May. Everybody appreciated his attentions, and he seemed to appreciate our attentions to him. Teach the boys to read, write and cipher? I never heard of, or saw that. There must be some mistake. He did not make much of what people call learning. But he gave us papers, books, and other such articles, too. In his habits he was very temperate. He did not smoke. People seemed to think it odd that he didn't, for everybody in Washington smoked. But he seemed to have a positive dislike for tobacco. He was a very moderate drinker. You might have thought something different, to see the ruddiness of his complexion — but his complexion had no whiskey in it. We might take a drink or two together occasionally — nothing more. It was our practice to go to a hotel on Washington Avenue after I was done with my car. I remember the place well —

INTERVIEW WITH PETER DOYLE

there on the corner. Like as not I would go to sleep — lay my head on my hands on the table. Walt would stay there, wait, watch, keep me undisturbed — would wake me up when the hour of closing came. In his eating he was vigorous, had a big appetite, but was simple in his tastes, not caring for any great dishes.

I never knew a case of Walt's being bothered up by a woman. In fact, he had nothing special to do with any woman except Mrs. O'Connor and Mrs. Burroughs. His disposition was different. Woman in that sense never came into his head. Walt was too clean, he hated anything which was not clean. No trace of any kind of dissipation in him. I ought to know about him those years — we were awful close together. In the afternoon I would go up to the Treasury building and wait for him to get through if he was busy. Then we'd stroll out together, often without any plan, going wherever we happened to get. This occurred days in and out, months running. Towards women generally Walt had a good way — he very easily attracted them. But he did that with men, too. And it was an irresistible attraction. I've had many tell me — men and women. He had an easy, gentle way — the same for all, no matter who they were or what their sex.

Walt was not at the theatre the night Lincoln was shot. It was me he got all that from in the book — they are almost my words. I heard that the President and his wife would be present and made up my mind to go.

CALAMUS

There was a great crowd in the building. I got into th
second gallery. There was nothing extraordinary in th
performance. I saw everything on the stage and was i
a good position to see the President's box. I heard th
pistol shot. I had no idea what it was, what it meant —
it was sort of muffled. I really knew nothing of what ha
occurred until Mrs. Lincoln leaned out of the box and crie
"The President is shot!" I needn't tell you what I fe
then, or saw. It is all put down in Walt's piece — tha
piece is exactly right. I saw Booth on the cushion of th
box, saw him jump over, saw him catch his foot, whic
turned, saw him fall on the stage. He got up on his fee
cried out something which I could not hear for the hu
hub and disappeared. I suppose I lingered almost th
last person. A soldier came into the gallery, saw me sti
there, called to me: "Get out of here! we're going t
burn this damned building down!" I said: "If that is s
I'll get out!"

We took great walks together — off towards or to Ale
andria, often. We went plodding along the road, Wa
always whistling or singing. We would talk of ordinar
matters. He would recite poetry, especially Shakespear
— he would hum airs or shout in the woods. He wa
always active, happy, cheerful, good-natured. Many c
our walks were taken at night. He never seemed to tir
When we got to the ferry opposite Alexandria I would sa
to myself, "I'll draw the line here — I won't go a ste
further." But he would take everything for granted —

INTERVIEW WITH PETER DOYLE

we would cross the river and walk back home on the other side. Walt knew all about the stars. He was eloquent when he talked of them. It was surprising what he knew of the operas, too, and the concerts of the Marine Band always tempted him. He never failed these concerts — we usually strayed in there together. The old man Scala led the band. He used to play a piece called "The Rival Birds" — Walt could get it off almost as good as the band.

He was a long time after me to go to New York, while his mother was alive. I asked him: "Will we stop there with your mother?" He was a little doubtful about that. We both stayed in Jersey City. The Whitmans lived on Portland Avenue. We took our dinner with Mrs. Whitman. We would take a bus-ride in the morning — then go to Brooklyn and have dinner. After we had had our dinner she would always say — "Now take a long walk to aid digestion." Mrs. Whitman was a lovely woman. There were just the three of us eating together. Walt and I had a week of it there in New York that time. It was always impressed upon my mind — the opera he took me to see — "Polyato." All the omnibus drivers knew him. We always climbed up to the top of the busses, our heels hanging over.

Yes, Walt often spoke to me of his books. I would tell him "I don't know what you are trying to get at." And this is the idea I would always arrive at from his reply. All other peoples in the world have had their representatives in literature: here is a great big race with no repre-

sentative. He would undertake to furnish that represen
tative. It was also his object to get a real human being
into a book. This had never been done before. These
were the two things he tried to impress upon me every
time we talked of books — especially of his books. Walt
used often to put a piece in Forney's Washington
Chronicle. We never really talked about politics. I was
a Catholic — am still supposed to be one. But I have
not been to church for so many years I would not know
what to do there. He had pretty vigorous ideas on
religion, but he never said anything slighting the church.
I don't know if he felt different from what he spoke. He
never went to church — didn't like form, ceremonies —
didn't seem to favor preachers at all. I asked him about
the hereafter. "There must be something," he said —
"there can't be a locomotive unless there is somebody to
run it." I have heard him say that if a person was a
right kind of person — and I guess he thought all persons
right kind of persons — he couldn't be destroyed in the
next world or this.

Dollars and cents had no weight with Walt at all. He
didn't spend recklessly, but he spent everything — mostly
on other people. Money was a thing he didn't think of
as other people thought of it. It came and went, that was
all there was to it. He did'nt buy many books, but I re
member that once he bought a set of Alexander Dumas
which afterward disappeared, I could not tell where
probably it was given away.

INTERVIEW WITH PETER DOYLE

I have Walt's raglan here [*goes to closet—puts it on*], I now and then put it on, lay down, think I am in the old times. Then he is with me again. It's the only thing I kept amongst many old things. When I get it on and stretched out on the old sofa I am very well contented. It is like Aladdin's lamp. I do not ever for a minute lose the old man. He is always near by. When I am in trouble — in a crisis — I ask myself, "What would Walt have done under these circumstances?" and whatever I decide Walt would have done that I do.

Walt's mood was very even, but I saw him mad as a March hare one night. He was on the hind end of my car, near him stood an old fellow (a carpet-bag senator — I don't know his name) — near-sighted, wore glasses, peevish, lantern-jawed, dyspeptic. They rubbed against each other. The first thing I knew there was a rumpus, the old man cussed Walt— said, "Get out of the way, you —" and Walt only answered: "Damn you!" The old man had a loaded stick with him — he raised it — would have struck Walt and perhaps killed him but I came between just in time. I cried: "Get in the car, Walt!" (they were both in the street by this time) and I was glad to see the affair ended that way. No explanations were made. All effects of it vanished at once from Walt's face and manner. Walt's temper was very even, it was a rare thing for him to get angry and he must have been greatly provoked. No man ever had better control over himself. He treated everybody fairly, generously. He wasn't meek, but he was no fighting-cock. He always had a few pennies for beggars along the street. I'd get out of patience sometimes, he was so lenient. "Don't you think its wrong?" I'd ask him. "No," he always said — "it's never wrong, Peter." Wouldn't they drink it away? He shook his head: "no, and if they did it wouldn't alter the matter. For it is better to give to a dozen who do not need what is given than to give to none at all and so miss the one that should be fed." Walt was kind to animals. He admired them, but he and animals never came to close quarters. His treatment of them was always generous. I never knew him cruel to man or beast. He had a dog once — Tip — in Camden, but he was not fond of animals for pets or especially glad to have them round him.

In Washington Walt told me he had made up his mind to celebrate the anniversary of the death of Lincoln every year. I have heard that he did it until his death. He called the thing a "religious duty." Do you remember the big black stick he carried even up to the last? I gave it to him. It delighted him. Gifts of that sort he always valued highly — the plainest, it might be, the most.

I once had the manuscript of "Drum Taps"; Walt made me a present of it. But somehow, when we moved, the manuscript disappeared — was either destroyed or stolen. Part of it was in print, but most of it was written. All his manuscript was pieced together in that fashion. At the time I did not appreciate it as I should now.

INTERVIEW WITH PETER DOYLE

Walt's manners were always perfectly simple. We would tackle the farmers who came into town, buy a water-melon, sit down on the cellar door of Bacon's grocery, Seventh & Pennsylvania Avenue, halve it and eat it. People would go by and laugh. Walt would only smile and say, "They can have the laugh — we have the melon."

You couldn't get a better idea of this simplicity than if I tell you of a visit paid him by Edmund Yates, in 1873, while he laid in the attic there in Washington, paralyzed, I being his nurse. Yates called and sent up his card. After some objections, mostly on my part, I referred the matter to Walt, who instantly said: "Admit him — let him come in." When Yates got into the room Walt saluted him by his first name and he addressed Walt as "Mr. Whitman." No two men were ever more different. Yates elegant, dressy, cultured — Walt plain, sick in bed, his room all littered and poor. But both men were perfectly at home. Yates did not seem fazed, Walt never was. In a few minutes they were in the midst of animated talk. When Yates, after awhile, got up and said: "Good bye" they seemed as if they had known each other many years.

Yes, Traubel, I know who it was Walt meant when he spoke to you of Grant's morning visits afoot to the old woman. Grant was then President. He would stroll from the White House alone. The woman he visited in this way was a widow, well known in Washington. Walt would laugh at me trying to get the President to ride — would motion Grant — he would shake his head. The later on we would see him at the widow's window outside, leaning on the sill. Grant was very fond of th old lady — in fact, she was much liked by men generally

Garfield and Walt were very good friends. Garfiel had a large manly voice; we would be going along th Avenue together — Walt and me — and we would hea Garfield's salutation at the rear. He always signalle Walt with the cry: "After all not to create only!" Whe we heard that we always knew who was coming. Garfiel would catch up and they would enter into a talk; I woul fall back sometimes. They spoke of books mainly bu of every other earthly thing also. Often they would no get through the first run and would go up and down th Avenue several times together — I was out of it. Ou tramping ground was between the Capitol and th Treasury.

Towards the end I saw very little of Walt, but he con tinued to write me. He never altered his manner towar me; here are a few more recent postal cards, you will se that they show the same old love. I know he wondere why I saw so little of him the three or four years befor he died, but when I explained it to him he understood Neverthless, I am sorry for it now. The obstacles wer too small to have made the difference I allowed. I was only this: In the old days I had always open door to Walt — going, coming, staying, as I chose. Now,

INTERVIEW WITH PETER DOYLE

had to run the gauntlet of Mrs. Davis and a nurse and what not. Somehow, I could not do it. It seemed as if things were not as they should have been. Then I had a mad impulse to go over and nurse him. I was his proper nurse — he understood me — I understood him. We loved each other deeply But there were things preventing that, too. I saw them. I should have gone to see him, at least, in spite of everything. I know it now, I did not know it then, but it is all right. Walt realized I never swerved from him — he knows it now — that is enough.

I have talked a long while. Let us drink up this beer together. It's a fearful warm day. You gentlemen take the glasses, there; I will drink right from the bottle. Now, here's to the dear old man and the dear old times — and the new times, too, and every one that's to come!

AMONG the men and women the multitude,
I perceive one picking me out by secret and divine signs,
Acknowledging none else, not parent, wife, husband, brother,
    child, any nearer than I am,
Some are baffled, but that one is not — that one knows me.

Ah lover and perfect equal,
I meant that you should discover me so by faint indirections,
And I when I meet you mean to discover you by the like in you
                    Leaves of Grass (Ed'n 1892), p. 111

LETTERS OF 1868

I

NEW YORK, *Friday*, 25 *Sept.*, 1868. DEAR BOY. I received your second letter yesterday—it is a real comfort to me to get such letters from you, dear friend. Every word does me good. The *Star* came all right, was quite interesting. I suppose you got my second letter last Wednesday. There is nothing new or special to write about to-day, still I thought I would send you a few lines for Sunday. I put down off hand and write all about myself and my doings, etc., because I suppose that will be really what my dear comrade wants most to hear while we are separated. I am doing a little literary work according as I feel in the mood — composing on my books. I am having a small edition of *Leaves of Grass* for 1867 fixed up and printed.* This and some other things give me

---

* *Drum-Taps* was published early in 1865. Then (upon Lincoln's assassination, 14 April) it was withdrawn from the market until *Sequel to Drum-Taps*, containing *When Lilacs Last in the Door-Yard Bloom'd* was ready. In 1867 an edition of *L. of G.* was published but these two sections were not included in it. Later in 1868, *Drum-Taps* and its sequel were incorporated into the *Leaves* but without change of the title page. It is this work of incorporation and the issue of a small edition of the thus reconstituted *L. of G.* which is referred to in the text.

CALAMUS

a little occupation. Upon the whole though I d(
do much but go around a great deal — eat my rati
every time — sleep at night like a top — and am hav
good times, so far, in a quiet way, enjoying New Y(
the society of my mother and lots of friends. An(
other things I spend a portion of the day with the pi]
of the ferry boats sailing on the river. The river ;
bay of New York and Brooklyn are always a great att
tion to me. It is a lively scene. At either flood or (
the water is always rushing along as if in haste, and
river is often crowded with steamers, ships and sn
craft moving in different directions, some coming fr
sea, others going out. Among the pilots are some of
particular friends — when I see them up in the p
house on my way to Brooklyn I go up and sail to ;
fro several trips. I enjoy an hour or two sail of this k
very much indeed. My mother and folks are well ;
are engaged just these times in the delightful business
moving. I should assist, but have hired a substitute
the shape of a stout young laboring man. I send you
mail a copy of the *Broadway* [Magazine] with the piec(
the same as I had in the car one day. It will not in
est you much only as something coming from me.
think of you very often, dearest comrade, and with m
calmness than when I was there. I find it first rate
think of you, Pete, and to know that you are there
right and that I shall return and we will be toget
again. I don't know what I should do if I hadn't you

LETTERS OF 1868

think of and look forward to. Tell Tom Hassett, on No,
7, that I wish to be remembered to him particular. Pete.
I hope this will find you entirely well of your cold. I am
glad to hear that your mother is all right of her cold. This
is the time of year when they are apt to be pretty trouble-
some. I should like to have seen that match played
between the Nationals and Olympic.

II

New York, 29 *Sept.*, 1868. DEAR BOY PETE. It is
splendid here to-day and I am feeling first rate. We
have had quite a dark and rainy spell, but now the prospect is good weather, clear sky, bright sun, coolish and
no dust. I shall spend an hour or two on the river to-
day. Your letter of the 27th, Sunday, came this morning. Also two *Stars*, 25th and 26th, the latter with
Hinton's speech, the other containing an item about me.
The previous *Star* arrived with your note of 23rd written
just as you were going to see the Black Crook—and next
morning another *Star* came. Peter, you are a good boy
and shall have your reward in heaven if not on earth.

Now how about that cold? I see you went to work
Saturday. You seem to be under the weather more than
I thought. Dear Comrade, I hope this will find you all right
and well as ever. I suppose you are working this week.
Yesterday I spent most of the day in Brooklyn helping
the folks to finish up the moving business. Got through

just after dark. I have not been to any amusements ye
Somehow I don't seem to care about them and I ;
around enough during the day. There is considerab
political excitement here — banners swung across tl
streets almost every block, and big transparencies in fro
of the different headquarters. I have seen several sple
did torch-light processions and out door meetings, etc.,
course the great majority in New York and Brooklyn
for Seymour and Blair.* I will now bid you good-b
for this time and God bless you, dear Comrade, and ke
you all right. Will write a line to No. 6. And w
speak to the other boys in my next.

III

New York, *Oct.* 2, 1868. DEAR BOY AND COMRAD
You say it is a pleasure to get my letters — well boy, it
a real pleasure to me to write to you. I just write, c
hand, whatever comes up, and, as I said before, most
about myself and my own doings. There have bee
some tremendous fires here — one in Brooklyn — eight
ten first class steam fire engines out — tell Harry on N
11 he would see quite a change in the fire department.
have more than I can attend to here. I find myself su
rounded by friends, many old ones, some new ones, son
young and attractive, and plenty of invitations and amus

* Democratic candidates for the presidency and vice-presidency
fall of '68.

LETTERS OF 1868

ments. I have received an invitation from a gentlemen and wife, friends of mine, at Providence, R. I., and shall go there and spend a few days latter part of October. How about the cold? I hope it is well. Dear Pete, with all my kind friends here and invitations, etc., though I love them all and gratefully reciprocate their kindness, I finally turn to you and think of you there. Well, I guess I have written enough for this time. Dear Pete, I will now bid you good-bye for the present. Take care of yourself and God bless you, my loving comrade. I will write again soon.

IV

Oct. 6, 1868. DEAR PETE. There is nothing special with me to write to you about. The time slips away mighty quick. It seems but a day or two since I left Washington yet am now on the fourth week of my furlough. Last night was about the greatest political show I ever saw even in New York — a grand Democratic meeting and torch light processions. I was out in the midst of them, to see the sights. I always enjoy seeing the City let loose and on the rampage as it was last night to the fullest extent. I cannot begin to tell you how the Democrats showed themselves by thousands and tens of thousands. The whole City was lit up with torches. Cannons were fired all night in various parts of the City. As I was on my way home in a 2nd Avenue car between 12 and 1 o'clock we got blocked in by a great part of the returning procession. Of course we had to just stand and take it. I enjoyed it hugely from the front platform They were nearly an hour passing us, streaming both sides. In the procession were all sorts of objects, model of ships forty or fifty feet long, full manned, cars o liberty with women, etc., etc. The ranks spread acros the street, and everybody carried a blazing torch. Fire works were going off in every direction. The sky wa full of big balloons letting off rockets and Roman candle 'way up among the stars. The excitement, the rush, an the endless torches gave me great pleasure. Ever an anon the cannon, some near some distant. I heard the long after I got to bed. It sounded like a distant engage ment. I send you the *Herald* with a sort of account o the show, but it doesn't do half justice to it.— Th speeches were of no account at all.

I suppose you got a letter and paper from me Saturday Oct. 3rd. I received your welcome letter of Oct. 1st also the *Star*. I read Mr. Noyes' western letters with pleasure. So you have something new in R. R.— new offices and rules. The R. R. [street railroad] busines here is very different. They go through these long route on the rush — no mercy to the cattle. The 3r Avenue R. R. lost 36 horses in one day last summer one of those hot days. We are having pleasant weathe just now, seems like Indian summer. So long, dea Pete. From your loving comrade, WALT.

LETTERS OF 1868

V

New York, Oct. 9, 1868. DEAR PETE. It is splendid here this forenoon — bright and cool. I was out early taking a short walk by the river only two squares from where I live. I received your letter last Monday, also the *Star* same date, and glad enough to hear from you and the oftener the better, every word is good (I am grateful to these young men on the R. R. for their love and remembrance to me — Dave and Jim and Charley Sorrell, Tom Hassett, Harry on No. 11). I sent you a letter on the 6th which I suppose you received next day. Tell Henry Hurt I received his letter of Oct. 5th all right, and that it was welcome. Political meetings here every night. The coming Pennsylvania and Ohio elections cause much talk and excitement. The fall is upon us; overcoats are in demand. I already begin to think about my return to Washington. A month has nearly passed away. I have received an invitation from a gentleman and his wife, friends of mine, at Providence, R. I., and shall probably go down there and spend a few days latter part of October. Shall I tell you about it or part of it just to fill up? I generally spend the forenoon in my room writing, etc., then take a bath fix up and go out about 12 and loafe somewhere or call on someone down town or on business, or perhaps if it is very pleasant and I feel like it ride a trip with some driver friend on Broadway from 23rd Street to Bowling Green, three

miles each way. (Every day I find I have plenty to d
every hour is occupied with something.) You know it
a never ending amusement and study and recreation f(
me to ride a couple of hours of a pleasant afternoon c
a Broadway stage in this way. You see everything :
you pass, a sort of living, endless panorama — sho|
and splendid buildings and great windows : and on tl
broad sidewalks crowds of women richly dressed co
tinually passing altogether different, superior in style ar
looks from any to be seen anywhere else — in fact a pe
fect stream of people — men too dressed in high styl
and plenty of foreigners — and then in the streets tl
thick crowd of carriages, stages, carts, hotel and priva
coaches, and in fact all sorts of vehicles and many fir
class teams, mile after mile, and the splendor of such
great street and so many tall, ornamental, noble buil
ings many of them of white marble, and the gayety ai
motion on every side : you will not wonder how muc
attraction all this is on a fine day, to a great loafer lil
me, who enjoys so much seeing the busy world mo
by him, and exhibiting itself for his amusement, while I
takes it easy and just looks on and observes. The
about the Broadway drivers, nearly all of them are n
personal friends. Some have been attached to me f
years and I to them. But I believe I have alrea(
mentioned them in a former letter. Yesterday I ro(
the trip I describe, with a friend on a 5th Avenue sta;
— No. 26, a sort [of] namesake of yours, Pete Calhoun,

have known him 9 or 10 years. The day was fine and I enjoyed the trip muchly. So I try to put in something in my letters to give you an idea of how I pass part of my time and what I see here in New York. Of course I have quite a variety. Some four or five hours every day I most always spend in study, writing, etc. The other serves for a good change. I am writing two or three pieces. I am having finished about 225 copies of *Leaves of Grass* bound up, to supply orders. Those copies form all that is left of the old edition. Then there will be no more in the market till I have my new and improved edition set up and stereotyped, which it is my present plan to do the ensuing winter at my leisure in Washington. Mother is well, I take either dinner or supper with her every day. Remember me to David Stevens and John Towers. Tell Harry on No. 11 I will go to the hall again and see if I can find that man in the Sheriff's office. I send you my love and *so long* for the present. Yours for life, dear Pete (and death the same).

VI

New York, Oct. 14, '68. DEAR BOY PETE. There is great excitement here over the returns of yesterday's elections, as I suppose there is the same in Washington also. The Democrats look blue enough and the Republicans are on their high horses. I suppose Grant's success is now certain. As I write the bands are out here

parading the streets and the drums beating. It is no
forenoon. To-night we will hear the big guns and s
the blazing bonfires. It is dark and cloudy weather he
to-day. I was glad to get your letter of Friday 9th whi
is the last -- also a *Star* at the same time. I suppose y
received mine of the 9th and the papers — the *Star* a
Express. I am about as well as usual. Mother is we
and my brothers the same. I am going to-morrow
Providence, R. I., to spend a few days. Should you wri
any time within four or five days after receiving th
direct to me *Care of Hon. Thomas Davis, Providence, R.*

My friend O'Connor is quite unwell and is absent fro
Washington away down on the New England Coast.
received a long letter from him yesterday. I believe
told you I was finishing up about 230 copies of my boo
expecting to sell them. I have had them finished up ar
bound, etc., but there is a hitch about the sale and
shall not be able to sell them at present. There is
pretty strong enmity here toward me and *L. of G.* amor
certain classes -- not only that it is a great mess of cra
talk and hard words all tangled up, without sense or mea
ing (which, by the by, is, I believe, your judgment about i
— but others sincerely think that it is a bad book, in
proper, and ought to be denounced and put down, and i
author along with it. There are some venomous b
laughable squibs occasionally in the papers. One sai
that I had received 25 guineas for a piece in an Engli
Magazine, but that it was worth all that for any one

read it. Another, the *World* said: "Walt Whitman was in town yesterday carrying the blue cotton umbrella of the future" (it had been a drizzly forenoon)—so they go it. When they get off a good squib however I laugh at it just as much as any one. Dear Pete, I hope this will find you well and in good spirits. Remember me to Coley, John Towers, Jim Sorrell, David Stevens and all the boys—WALT.

I have been debating whether to get my leave extended and stay till election day to vote or whether to pair off with a Democrat and return (which will amount to the same thing). Most likely I shall decide on the latter, but don't know for certain. Dear boy, I send you my love— I will write you a line from Providence — so long — Pete.

VII

Providence, R. I., Oct. 17, 1868. DEAR PETE. According to announcement in my last I have made a movement and change of base from tumultuous, close-packed, world-like New York to this half-rural, brisk, handsome, New England, third-class town. I came on here last Thursday. I came as guest of Thomas Davis, formerly M. C. from this City — Arrived between 8 and 9 o'clock at night — found his carriage at the depot waiting for me. At the house — a sort of castle built of stone, on fine grounds, a mile and a half from the town — a hearty welcome from his hospitable wife and a family of young

CALAMUS

ladies and children — a hot supper — a tip top room, etc
etc.,— so you see, Pete, your old man is in clover. I hav
since been round the City and suburbs considerably.
am going down to Newport before I return — Invitation
etc., are numerous — I am, in fact, already dividing my
self between two hospitalities, part of the time with M
and Mrs. Davis and part with Dr. and Mrs. Channing
old acquaintances of mine in another part of the City
I stopt last night at the house of the latter. It is on
high and pleasant hill at the side of the City which it entirel
overlooks. From the window of my room I can loo
down across the city, the river, and off miles upon mile
in the distance. The woods are a real spectacle, colore
with all the rich colors of autumn. Yesterday it wa
beautiful and balmy beyond description, like the fines
Indian summer. I wandered around, partly walking
partly in a carriage, a good part of the day. To-day ther
is an entire change of scene. As I am writing this, wha
do you think, Pete? great flakes of snow are falling —
quite a thick flurry — sometimes the wind blows in gust
— in fact a real snow storm has been going on all th
forenoon, though without the look or feeling of winter a
the grass and foliage are autumnal and the cold is no
severe yet. Still it [is] disagreeable and wet and darl
and prevents me from going out. So I will make up b
writing a couple of letters, one to mother and one to you
telling you about things. Providence is a handsome cit
of about 70,000 inhabitants, has numerous manufactorie

in full operation — everything looks lively. From the house up here I can hear almost any time, night or day, the sound of factory bells and the steam whistles of locomotives half a mile distant. Then the lights at night seen from here make a curious exhibition. At both places I stop we have plenty of ripe fresh fruit and lots of flowers. Pete, I could now send you a bouquet every morning far better than I used to — of much choicer flowers. And how are you getting along, dearest comrade? I hope you are well and that everything is going on right with you. I have not heard from you for a good while, it seems. I suppose you got my last letter of 14th, from N. Y. I expect to return to N. Y. about the 22nd. Should you feel to write after receiving this you might direct to 331 East 55th Street as before. I am well as usual. I am luxuriating on excellent grapes. I wish I could send you a basket. At both places I stop they have vineyards and the grapes are very good and plenty this year. Last night when I went up at 11 o'clock to my room I took up three great bunches each as big as my fist and sat down and eat them before I turned in. I like to eat them in this way and it agrees with me. It is quite a change here from my associations and surroundings either in Washington or New York. Evenings and meal times I find myself thrown amidst a mild, pleasant society, really intellectual, composed largely of educated women, some young, some not so young, everything refined and polite, *not* disposed to small talk, conversing in earnest on profound subjects,

CALAMUS

but with a moderate rather slow tone and in a kind
conciliatory manner — delighting in this sort of convers
tion and spending their evenings till late, in it. I take
hand in, for a change. I find it entertaining, as I sa
for novelty's sake, for a week or two — but I know ve
well that would be enough for me. It is all first ra
good and smart but too constrained and bookish for
free old hawk like me. I send you my love, dear Pe
So long. Will write from N. Y. soon as I return the
P. S. Just after 12 o'clock noon. As I am just finis
ing the storm lightens up — I am sure I see a bit of bl
sky in the clouds — yes, the sun is certainly breaki
out.

VIII

Providence, R. I., Oct. 18, '68. DEAR BOY AND CO
RADE, I sent off a letter to you yesterday noon, b
towards evening Mr. Davis brought me up from the
O. yours of 15th, which I was so glad to get that y
shall have an answer right off. After the flurry of sn
I told you of yesterday morning we had a pleasant cle
afternoon. I took a long walk, partly through the woo
and enjoyed it much. The weather, pretty cold and sha
and remains so yet. As I left my overcoat in Washir
ton I have been compelled to get something here, sc
have bought me a great iron grey shawl which I find ve
acceptable. I always had doubts about a shawl, but ha
already got used to mine and like it first rate. In t

evening I went by invitation to a party of ladies and gentlemen — mostly ladies. We had a warm, animated talk, among other things about spiritualism. I talked too, indeed went in like a house afire. It was good exercise — for the fun of the thing. I also made love to the women, and flatter myself that I created at least one impression — wretch and gay deceiver that I am. The truth is Peter, that I am here at the present time mainly in the midst of female women, some of them young and jolly, and meet them most every evening in company, and the way in which this aged party comes up to the scratch and cuts out the youthful parties and fills their hearts with envy is absolutely a caution. You would be astonished, my son, to see the brass and coolness and the capacity of flirtation and carrying on with the girls — I would never have believed it of myself. Brought here by destiny, surrounded in this way and, as I in self defense would modestly state, sought for, seized upon and ravenously devoured by these creatures — and so nice and smart some of them are, and handsome too — there is nothing left for me, is there, but to go in. Of course, young man, you understand it is all on the square. My going in amounts to just talking and joking and having a devil of a jolly time carrying on — that's all. They are all as good girls as ever lived. I have already had three or four such parties here — which you will certainly admit, considering my age and heft, to say nothing of my reputation, is doing pretty well. Then away late — lost my way — wandered over the City and got home after on o'clock.

I go about quite a good deal. This is as handsome City as I ever saw, some of the streets run up steep hill: Except in a few of the business streets, where the build ings are compact — in nine-tenths of the City — ever house stands separate and has a little or quite a deal c ground about it for flowers and for shade or fruit trees c a garden. I never saw such a prosperous looking Cit — but of course no grand public buildings like Wasl ington.

This forenoon I have been out away down along th banks of the river and cove and making exploration generally. All is new to me and I returned quite tirec I have eat a hearty dinner. Then I thought I woul come up and sit awhile in my room. But as I did nc feel like reading I concluded to write this precious screec Fortunate young man, to keep getting such instructiv letters — aint you? It is now four o'clock and bright an cool and I have staid in long enough. I will sally fort on a walk and drop this in the P. O. before supper. S long, dear Pete, and my love to you as always, alway: WALT.

IX

New York — Oct. 22nd (?) 1868. DEAR PETE — Wel here I am back again in New York. Have had pleasant trip down East — went down the bay there afte

LETTERS OF 1868

I wrote you last and also a visit around among the factories of Rhode Island. Some of them are very large — regular little towns. The Spragues, two brothers, employ 7000 workmen in their factories alone. Some of the owners are men of immense wealth. I write this early in the forenoon sitting in my room in 55th street after breakfast. As to getting my leave extended so that I might stay to vote, I have settled (as I spoke of in a former letter) to pair off with a friend of mine here who was going to vote for Seymour and return on time. The weather is cool and clear to-day. I shall probably not make out much of a letter to you this time, Pete, as I feel rather stupid yet this morning. I guess I slept too hard or perhaps, as they say, I got up wrong end foremost. But I thought I would write one more letter for the last. I hope you have enjoyed reading them as much as I have writing them — for that I *have* enjoyed. You too have done first rate and have sent me as many as I have you, and good letters too. I am now going out down town and across to Brooklyn to spend a few hours with my mother. I don't know whether I told you that my sister with her two young children from St. Louis arrived the night before I left New York, and will stop with mother this fall and winter — her health* is not very good. I shall return 26th — Take care of yourself, Dear Pete, we will soon be together again — WALT.

* *i. e.* the health of the "sister" (Jeff's wife Mattie) — she died of consumption 19th Feb. 1873.

I WILL plant companionship thick as trees along all the rivers of
 America, and along the shores of the great lakes, and all
 over the prairies,
I will make inseparable cities with their arms about each other's
 necks,
   By the love of comrades,
   By the manly love of comrades.
                              Leaves of Grass (Ed'n 1892), p. 99.

LETTERS OF 1869

1

BROOKLYN, N. Y., *Saturday evening, Aug.* 21 [1869]. DEAR PETE. I have been very sick the last three days—I don't know what to call it—it makes me prostrated and deadly weak, and little use of my limbs. I have thought of you, my darling boy, very much of the time. I have not been out of the house since the first day after my arrival. I had a pleasant journey through on the cars Wednesday afternoon and night—felt quite well then. My mother and folks are all well. We are in our new house— we occupy part and rent out part. I have a nice room, where I now sit writing this. It is the latter part of the afternoon. I feel better the last hour or so. It has been extremely hot here the last two days—I see it has been so in Washington too. I hope I shall get out soon—I hanker to get out doors, and down the bay. And now dear Pete for yourself. How is it with you, dearest boy—and is there anything different with the face?* Dear Pete, you must forgive me for being so

---

* At this time Doyle was suffering from an eruption on his face of which he did not know the cause. Whitman took him to Dr. Charles Bowen, one of the army doctors, who pronounced it a case of "barber's itch" (tinea sycosis), an exceedingly obstinate skin

CALAMUS

cold the last day and evening. I was unspeakabl
shocked and repelled from you by that talk and proposi
tion of yours — you know what — there by the fountain
It seemed indeed to me, (for I will talk out plain to you
dearest comrade) that the one I loved, and who ha(
always been so manly and sensible, was gone, and a foc
and intentional suicide stood in his place. I spoke s
sternly and cutting. (Though I see now that my word
might have appeared to have a certain other meaning
which I didn't dream of — insulting to you, never for on
moment in my thoughts.) But will say no more of thi
— for I know such thoughts must have come when yo
was not yourself but in a moment of derangement, — an(
have passed away like a bad dream. Dearest boy I hav
not a doubt but you will get well and entirely well — an(
we will one day look back on these drawbacks and suffer
ings as things long past. The extreme cases of tha
malady, (as I told you before) are persons that have ver
deeply diseased blood so they have no foundation to buil(
on — you are of healthy stock, with a sound constitutio

disease, which he said could best be eradicated by lancing and cav
terizing with nitrate of silver. At Doyle's solicitation Dr. Bowe
undertook the treatment at once, but for a time no improvemer
was apparent. In a moment of despondency Doyle declared tha
life burdened with such an affliction was not worth living. Whi
man took this thoughtless speech too literally as appears from th
letter, and it is in perfect keeping with his imperturbable faith an
complete acceptance of life that he should have been shocked, as h
was, by even a suggestion of suicide.

and good blood — and I know it is impossible for it to continue long. My darling, if you are not well when I come back I will get a good room or two in some quiet place, and we will live together and devote ourselves altogether to the job of curing you, and making you stronger and healthier than ever. I have had this in my mind before but never broached it to you. I could go on with my work in the Attorney General's office just the same — and we would see that your mother should have a small sum every week to keep the pot a-boiling at home. Dear comrade, I think of you very often. My love for you is indestructible, and since that night and morning has returned more than before. Dear Pete, dear son, my darling boy, my young and loving brother, don't let the devil put such thoughts in your mind again — wickedness unspeakable — death and disgrace here, and hell's agonies hereafter — Then what would it be afterward to the mother? What to *me?* — Pete, I send you some money by Adams' Express — you use it, dearest son, and when it is gone you shall have some more, for I have plenty. I will write again before long — give my love to Johnny Lee, my dear darling boy. I love him truly — (let him read these three last lines) — Dear Pete, *remember* — WALT.

II

Brooklyn, September 3, 1869. DEAR PETE. I thought I would write you a letter to-day, as you would be anxious to hear. I received your letter of Aug. 24, and it was a great comfort to me. I have read it several times since. Dear Pete, I hope everything is going on favorably with you. I think about you every day and every night. I do hope you are in good spirits and health. I want to hear about the face. I suppose you are working on the road. There is nothing new or special in my affairs or doings. The weather is pleasant here — it is pretty cool and dry. My folks all continue well — mother first rate, and brothers ditto. I do not have such good luck, I have felt unwell most every day — some days not so bad. Besides I have those spells again, worse, last longer, sick enough, come sudden, dizzy and sudden sweat — It is hard to tell exactly what is the matter or what to do. The doctor says it is all from that hospital malaria, hospital poison absorbed in the system years ago — he thinks it better for me in Washington than here. About one third of the time I feel pretty well. I have taken three or four of my favorite rides on Broadway, I believe I described them to you in my letters a year ago. I find many of my old friends, and new ones too, and am received with the same warm friendship and love as ever. Broadway is more crowded and gay than ever, and the women look finer, and the shops richer — then there are many new and splendid buildings of marble or iron — they seem to almost reach the clouds, they are so tall — some of them cost millions of dollars. Staging in N. Y. has been very poor this summer — $9 or $10 even on the big

Broadway lines — Railroading has also been slim. New York is all cut up with railroads — Brooklyn also — I have seen Jimmy Foy — he was over to Brooklyn looking for work on a road. He was well and hearty, and wished to be remembered to you. They pay $2½ on many of the roads here and 2¼ on the rest. The work is pretty hard, but the hours not so long as in Washington. There is all kinds of fun and sport here, by day and night — and lots of theatres and amusements in full blast. I have not been to any of them — have not been to see any of my particular women friends — though sent for (the papers here have noticed my arrival) — have not been down to the sea-shore as I intended.— In fact my jaunt this time has been a failure — Better luck next time — Now Pete, dear loving boy, I don't want you to worry about me — I shall come along all right. — As it is, I have a good square appetite most of the time yet, good nights' sleep — and look about the same as usual, (which is of course lovely and fascinating beyond description). Tell Johnny Lee I send him my love, and hope he is well and hearty. I think of him daily. 1 sent him a letter some time ago, which I suppose he received about Aug. 26, and showed you — but I have not had a word from him. Send him this letter to read, as he will wish to hear about me. God bless you, dear Pete — dear loving comrade, and farewell till next time, my darling boy. WALT.

CALAMUS

III

Brooklyn, Friday afternoon, Sept. 10, 1869. DEA[R]
PETE—DEAR SON. I have received your letter of the 8t[h]
to-day — all your letters have come safe — four alto[-]
gether. This is the third I have sent you (besides th[e]
one by Adams' Express, Aug. 23rd). Pete, you say m[y]
sickness must be worse than I described in my letters –
and ask me to write precisely how I am. No, deare[st]
boy, I wrote just as it really was. But Pete, you will no[w]
be truly happy to learn that I am feeling all right, an[d]
have been mainly so for the last four days,— and hav[e]
had no bad spells all that time. Yesterday I thought [I]
felt as strong and well as ever in my life — in fact re[al]
young and jolly. I loafed around New York most a[ll]
day — had a first rate good time. All along Broadwa[y]
hundreds of rich flags and streamers at half-mast fo[r]
Gen. Rawlins'* funeral. From the tall buildings the[y]
waved out in a stiff west wind all across Broadway — lat[e]
in the afternoon I rode up from the Battery to look a[t]
them,— as the sun struck through them —I thought [I]
had never seen anything so curious and beautiful. O[f]
all the shipping, ferry boats, public buildings, etc., flag[s]

---

* John Aaron Rawlins, b. at East Galena, Ill., 13 Feb. '31, d. [at]
Washington, D. C., 9 Dec., '69. A General in the Northern arm[y.]
Was a Douglas democrat in '60, but joined the Union Army on th[e]
outbreak of the Civil War and became Assistant Adjutant Gener[al]
to Grant in 1861 and Chief of Staff with the rank of Brigadier Gener[al]
in 1865. Was Secretary of War 1869.

at half-mast too. This is the style here. No black drapery for mourning — only thousand of flags at half mast, on the water as well as land — for any big bug's funeral. To-day I am all right too. It is now towards 3 — mother and I have just had our dinner, (my mammy's own cooking mostly,) I have been out all the forenoon knocking around — the water is my favorite recreation — I could spend two or three hours every day of my life here, and never get tired — some of the pilots are dear personal friends of mine — some, when we meet we kiss each other (I am an exception to all their customs with others,) — some of their boys have grown up since I have known them, and they too know me and are very friendly.— Pete, the fourth week of my vacation is most ended. I shall return the middle of next week. Give my love to Johnny Lee — let him read this letter and then return it to you. Dear Jack, I received your affectionate letter of Sept. 5th. Pete, I have seen Tom Haslett — he is well — he is working extra on Broadway and 42nd St. R. R. He does not think of going home till Christmas. Jimmy Foy has not got work yet. I suppose you got "Kenilworth" I sent. Well, boy, I shall now take a bath, dress myself and go out, cross the river, put this letter in the P. O. and then ramble and ride around the City awhile, as I think we are going to have a fine evening and moonlight, etc. Good-bye, dear son — we will soon be together again. WALT.

WHAT think you I take my pen in hand to record?
The battleship, perfect model'd, majestic, that I saw pass the
    offing today under full sail?
The splendors of the past day? or the splendor of the night that
    envelops me?
Or the vaunted glory and growth of the great city spread around
    me?—no;
But merely of two simple men I saw today on the pier in the
    midst of the crowd, parting the parting of dear friends,
The one to remain hung on the other's neck and passionately
    kissed him,
While the one to depart tightly prest the one to remain in his
    arms.

Leaves of Grass (Ed'n 1892), p. 110.

LETTERS OF 1870

I

BROOKLYN, *Saturday afternoon, July* 30 [1870]. DEAR PETE. Well here I am home again with my mother, writing to you from Brooklyn once more. We parted there, you know, at the corner of 7th St. Tuesday night. Pete there was something in that hour from 10 to 11 o'clock (parting though it was) that has left me pleasure and comfort for good — I never dreamed that you made so much of having me with you, nor that you could feel so downcast at losing me. I foolishly thought it was all on the other side. But all I will say further on the subject is, I now see clearly, that was all wrong. I started from the depot in the 7.25 train the next morning — it was pretty warm, yet I had a very pleasant journey, and we got in New York by 5 o'clock afternoon. About half an hour before we arrived, I noticed a very agreeable change in the weather — the heat had moderated — and in fact it has been pleasant enough every day since. I found mother and all as well as usual. It is now Saturday between 4 and 5 in the afternoon — I will write more on the other side — but Pete, I must now hang up for the present as there is a young lady down stairs whom I have to go with to the ferry and across to the cars.

CALAMUS

Sunday, 6 p. m. Pete, dear boy, I will write you a line to-day before I go. I am going over to New York to visit the lady I went down to the ferry with — so you see I am quite a lady's man again in my old days — There is nothing special to write about — I am feeling in first-rate spirits and eat my rations every time. *Monday, Aug. 1* The carrier brought quite a bunch this forenoon for the Whitman family, but no letter from you. I keep real busy with one thing and another, the whole day is occupied — I am feeling quite well all the time and go out a great deal, knocking around one place and another The evenings here are delightful and I am always out in them, sometimes on the river sometimes in New York — There is a cool breeze and the moon shining. I think every time of you and wish if we could only be together these evenings at any rate. *Tuesday, Aug. 2.* Well Pete, you will have quite a diary at this rate. Your letter came this morning — and I was glad enough to get word from you. I have been over to New York to-day on business — it is a pleasure even to cross the ferry — the river is splendid to-day — a stiff breeze blowing and the smell of the salt sea blowing up — (sweeter than any per fume to my nose) — It is now 2 o'clock, I have had my dinner and am sitting here alone writing this — Love to you, dear Pete — and I won't be so long again writing to — my darling boy. WALT.

LETTERS OF 1870

II

Brooklyn, Wednesday night, Aug. 3, [1870]. DEAR
PETE. Dear son, I received your second letter to-day —
also the Star. I sent you a letter Tuesday evening, which
I suppose you have received. As I am now sitting in my
room and have no desire to go to bed yet, I will commence
another. Give my best respects to George Smith — also
to Pensey Bell and his brother George — also to Mr.
Shedd — and in fact to all my railroad friends whenever
they enquire after me — Dear son, I can almost see you
drowsing and nodding since last Sunday, going home late
— especially as we wait there at 7th St. and I am telling
you something deep about the heavenly bodies — and in
the midst of it I look around and find you fast asleep, and
your head on my shoulder like a chunk of wood — an
awful compliment to my lecturing powers. All the talk
here now is either the war on the Rhine, or the murder
of old Mr. Nathan, or some other murder — for there are
plenty of them — I send you a couple of papers with
pieces about them. Say whether they come safe. I
believe that is all for to-night, as it is getting late. Good
night, Pete — Good night, my darling son — here is a kiss
for you, dear boy — on the paper here — a good long
one. *Thursday* — *4th* — I have been out all the forenoon
and until about 2 o'clock — had some business in New
York, which I attended, then came back and spent an
hour and a half on the river, with one of the pilots, a

CALAMUS

particular friend of mine — saw the yachts, several of
them, including the America, out practising for the great
race that comes off Monday — the Dauntless was ou
yesterday — and the Cambria went down three days ag
— the America is the handsomest little craft I ever lai
eyes on — I also saw Henry Ward Beecher and had som
talk with him — I find myself going with the pilots much
— there are several that were little boys, now grown u
and remember me well — fine hearty fellows — alway
around the water — sons of old pilots — they make muc
of me, and of course I am willing. 10 *o'clock at nig*
— As this is lying here on my table to be sent off to-mo
row, I will imagine you with your arm around my nec
saying Good night, Walt — and me — Good night, Pete.-
Friday morning, *Aug*. 5. — All well — fine weather and
feel in good spirits. I am just going out and across
to New York. We had a heavy shower here yesterd:
afternoon 4th, the weather is not too hot here. WALT.

III

Brooklyn, *August* 7, [1870]. DEAR BOY PETE. It is
beautiful quiet Sunday forenoon. I am feeling first ra
and have had quite a good day so far. After breakfast
went out and sat a long while on the porch in front, readir
the Sunday paper, enjoying the cool and shade, — ar
besides some real sweet music — A young widow ne
door, a friend of mother's, has been in her parlor the la

three hours, singing and practising — she has a voice not powerful and ornamental as the opera ladies, but with that something, pleasing and tender, that goes to the right spot — sings good old hymns and songs — I have enjoyed it greatly — you would too — It is now between 1-2 past 10 and 11 — The distant bells are slowly ringing — otherwise it is pretty quiet — The last two hours I have been up here reading my proof. I have four or five hours of this every day, which gives me something to do — an employment like. Pete, I have just taken out your last letter and read it over again — I went out on a kind of little excursion by myself last night — all alone — It was very pleasant, cool enough and the moon shining — I think of you too, Pete, and a great deal of the time. *Tuesday afternoon, 9th*, I was out yesterday a great part of the day on the river to see the yacht race — over a thousand spectator boats, big, little, and middle sized — many of them all drest with flags, bright colored streamers, etc. streaming over the green waters, beneath the sunshine and bright blue sky — a grand sight — and the beautiful yachts and pleasure boats, lots and lots of them, with immense white sails, like great wings, tearing along in the breeze — the bay each side alive with people on the boats — 150,000 people they say — the shores and hills covered for miles too — I was out again last night. It was fine. — Your welcome letter of the 8th has come this morning, dear loving son, and has pleased me, as always. That accident on the bridge was indeed terrible

— that bridge is a disgrace to Washington, anyhow -
Pete, I wish you to tell Mr. and Mrs. Nash and you
cousin, and all, I send them my best respects — Als
Henry Hurt, also Andy Woolbridge on 7th St. *Wedne
day afternoon*, 10*th*. Dear son. Yours of 9th, can
this forenoon — I feel quite unhappy about your bad luc
again — reported by some damned fool, and taken off b
a worse damned fool — But you keep a good heart, Pe
— school will keep somehow — I have no room to wri
more at present — Dear loving son, I want to keep wri
ing frequently. WALT. Just going out — But just in tl
nick of time before I sealed this letter as I had finishe
dressing to go out, Mother sung out to me from the fo
of the stairs — and I got your good welcome third lette
Pete, you are doing first rate. I guess Pleasants w:
after something stronger than Kissengen — Tell Dr. Mi
burn I don't find any place in N. Y. or Brooklyn to cor
pare with his for the mineral drinks — But I am livir
more to suit me in the grub line, this weather — not s
much meat — mother's cookery, and quite a good deal
fruit, etc. — A lovely broiled steak and perfect coffee th
morning — I wish you had been on hand, young man.

IV

Brooklyn, August 12, [1870]. DEAR SON. Yours
yesterday 11th, has just this minute come, and I wish
write a few lines so that you may get them before Sur

day. I have not time to write much, as it is now about 5 P. M. Dear son, I hope you will not feel discouraged at the situation, even if it comes to the worst. It is now thought that business generally throughout the country is ready to revive as soon as the hot season is done, and that everything will be brisker this fall than any time since the war. Dear Pete, whatever happens, in such ups and downs, you must try to meet it with a stout heart. As long as the Almighty vouchsafes you health, strength, and a clear conscience, let other things do their worst,— and let Riker go to hell. You are better off to-day to be what you are, than to be him with his $10,000 a year — poor thin-livered cuss that he is.— My darling son, I will send you $5 every Saturday, should you be idle — as I can easily spare that, and you can depend upon it — it won't go far, but it may take the edge off. Many, many loving kisses to you, dear son— for I must close, or I shall lose to-night's mail. WALT.

V

Brooklyn, August 22, 1870. DEAR PETE. I have not heard from you now for nine days. Your letter of 13th, (last Saturday week) in which you said the orders were for you to go to work next day, was the last I have received. I took it for granted that you went to work, and have been at it since — and I hope all is right with you — but why have you not written? — Dear son, if not

CALAMUS

to work I wish to send you a little money. Everythin[g]
goes well with me — that is, everything goes as well [as]
can be expected — I am feeling first-rate — I am dow[n]
the bay often, and sometimes spend nearly all day [on]
the sea-shore a few miles down. I am all sunburnt an[d]
red, and weigh several pounds more than when I le[ft]
Washington. A friend who hasn't seen me for a goo[d]
while said this morning— "Why Walt, you are fatter an[d]
saucier than ever"— but I will close by sending my lo[ve]
to my darling son — and to him I shall always be t[he]
same old WALT.

VI

Brooklyn, August 25 [1870]. DEAR SON. I will beg[in]
a letter for you to-day, and probably finish it to-morro[w]
and send it off, so that you will have it by or before Su[n]
day. The heat is again upon us here, days — but t[he]
nights are pleasant. It is now Thursday afternoon, b[e]
tween 3 and 4 — and I am writing this in my room o[n]
Portland Ave. Pete, one month of my leave exactly [is]
up to-day. I have been out quite a while to-day over [to]
New York, to the printing office, and seeing to one thin[g]
and another. It was sweaty work. On my way back [I]
went up in the pilot house and sailed across the riv[er]
three times— a fine breeze blowing. Then home — too[k]
a bath — ate my dinner— and here I am all alone mo[stly]
stript, taking things as cool as possible, and writing th[is]
letter. Pete, your letter of 23rd came yesterday, and t[he]

LETTERS OF 1870

one written partly that night and partly 24th came this forenoon. Those are the only letters I have received since the one of 13th telling me the orders were for you to go to work next day (Sunday). I have been uneasy ever since to hear. The letter received this morning gives me the first definite information how things have turned out. Dear son, I want you to try to cast aside all irritating thoughts and recollections, and preserve a cheerful mind. That is the main part of getting along through the toil and battle of life — and it is a good deal habit. I was away a good part of last week down the bay — went away each time early in the morning, and got home after dark. I am having quite jovial times. I went to Wallack's theatre one night lately with a friend who wanted to see a piece called "Fritz" — a miserable sickish piece. I was glad enough to get out in the open air away from such humbug. I am still feeling gay and hearty. I work several hours a day keeping things straight among the printers and founders on my books. They are being cast in electrotype plates.* I will tell you more about it when we meet. Well Pete, I guess this will do for to-day. I think of sallying forth soon as the sun gets pretty well down, and crossing to New York to loafe around two or three hours. *Friday afternoon, August* 26. Well I went over to New York last evening — up town to see some friends — come home about 11 — just in

* These plates were used for the 1871-'72 and '76 eds. of *Leaves of Grass*.

time to escape a thunder shower. It is splendid to-day —
I have been over all day working, quite busy — and have
just got home, and had my dinner — it is now about 4
It is quite pleasant riding here in Brooklyn — we have
large open cars, in good weather it is real lively — I quite
enjoy it — Pete, give my respects to Mr. and Mrs. Nash
and to your cousin — also to Jenny Murphy — not forget
ting the boys on the road — also Wash Milburn — God
bless you — and good-bye for this time, my own dear lov
ing boy. WALT.

VII

Brooklyn, September 2, 1870. DEAR PETE. I receive
your welcome letter of Aug. 27th and also 31st, enclos
ing Ned Stewart's — when you write tell Ned I am her
in Brooklyn, loafing around — and that I send my love
Pete, there is nothing particular to write about this tim
— pretty much the same story — every day out on th
bay awhile, or going down to Coney Island beach — an
every day from two to four or five hours in the printin
office — I still keep well and hearty, and the weather i
fine — warm through the middle of the day, and coo
morning and nights — I fall in with a good many of m
acquaintances of years ago — the young fellows, (no
not so young) — that I knew intimately here before th
war — some are dead — and some have got married —
and some have grown rich — one of the latter I was u
with yesterday and last night — he has a big house o

Fifth Avenue I was there to — dinner (dinner at 8
P. M.!) — everything in the loudest sort of style, with
wines, silver, nigger waiters, etc. etc. etc. But my friend
is just one of the manliest, jovialest, best sort of fellows —
no airs, and just the one to suit you and me,— no women
in the house — he is single — he wants me to make my
home there — I shall not do that, but shall go there very
frequently — the dinners and good wines are attractive — then there is a fine library. Well Pete, I am on
the second month of my furlough — to think it is almost
six weeks since we parted there that night — my dear
loving boy, how much I want to see you — it seems a
long while. I have received a good letter from Mr.
O'Connor, and also one from John Rowland who is in
the office for me. Nothing new in office — Well, Pete,
about half of our separation is over — the next six weeks
will soon pass away — indeed it may be only four, as John
Rowland told me he might wish to go away — Good-bye
for the present, my loving son, and give my respects to
any of the boys that ask about me. WALT.

VIII

Brooklyn, September 6th, 1870. DEAR SON. I see by
your letter of the 4th, that you are working as usual. I
sometimes fancy I see you — and 14*— and Mr. Shedd

* "14" was the number of the street car of which Pete was
conductor at this time and is used as a name for the car by Whitman. Mr. Shedd was the driver on "14".

CALAMUS

going up or down the avenue — or at the end at Georgetown — or Navy Yard — the old familiar route and scenes — the circle, the President's House — Willards' — 7th Street — Capitol Gate — the Hill, etc. etc. etc. I keep pretty busy, writing, proof-reading, etc. I am at the printing office several hours every day — I feel in capital health and spirits — weigh several pound heavier — but, as a small drawback, and something new for me, find myself needing glasses every time I read or write* — this has grown upon me very rapidly since and during the hot weather, and especially since I left Washington — so I read and write as little as possible, beyond my printing matters, etc. — as that occupies several hours and tires my eyes sometimes. We are having splendid fall weather, both days and nights. Last night I was out late — the scene on the river was heavenly — the sky clear, and the moon shining her brightest — I felt almost chilly at last with the cold — and so put for home. One of the prettiest sights now is to see the great German steamers, and other ships, as they lay tied up along shore, all covered with gay flags and streamers — " dress ship " as they call it — flaunting out in the breeze, under a brilliant sky and sun — all in honor, of course, of the victory of the German Armies — all the spars and rigging are hid with hundreds and hundreds of flags — a big red, white and black flag capping all. Of course you may

* He was in his 52d year. The average age to begin wearing glasses is about forty-five.

know that the way the war turns out suits me to death — Louis Napoleon fully deserves his fate — I consider him by far the meanest scoundrel (with all his smartness) that ever sat on a throne. I make a distinction, however, I admire and love the French, and France as a nation — of all foreign nations, she has my sympathy first of all. Pete, I was just reading over your last letter again. Dear son, you must try to keep up a good heart. You say you do — but I am afraid you are feeling, (or have felt,) somewhat unhappy. One soon falls into the habit of getting low spirited or deprest and moody — if a man allows himself, he will always find plenty to make him so — Everyone [has] his trouble, disappointments, rebuffs, etc. especially every young and proud-spirited man who has to work for his living. But I want you to try and put a brave face against everything that happens — for it is not so much the little misfortunes of life themselves, as the way we take them and brood over them, that causes the trouble. About the "tiresome" all I have to say is — to say nothing — only a good smacking kiss and many of them — and taking in return many, many, many, from my dear son — good loving ones too — which will do more credit to his lips than growling and complaining at his father. WALT.

IX

Brooklyn, September 9, 1870. DEAR SON. I wrote you a letter last Tuesday, 6th, which I suppose you have received. The last I have from you is yours of Sunday 4th. I am still here in Brooklyn, quite busy with the printing. I have received a letter from John Rowland who is working for me in the office, complaining that he has to work too hard,—I should think by his letter he means to back out of his bargain with me—if so, it will be a bad loss and inconvenience to me—But I shall not fret about it whatever happens. It is likely that this will shorten my leave, and that I shall have to come back and do my work myself, about the end of the month Dear Pete, I hope you are having good times, and are in good spirits. We are having quite coolish weather here The drivers wear their over-coats mornings and evenings As I sit here writing Friday afternoon, it is cloudy and threatens rain. I am going over to New York in an hour or so, and shall leave this in the P. O. and then go around awhile—possibly going to Niblo's Theatre, as they play Shakespeare's "Julius Cæsar" to-night, with Davenport and quite a bunch of stars in the piece. Son I am afraid I shall not make out much of a letter this time, but you take it so hard when I don't write, I thought I would send a few lines—they would be better than nothing. God bless you, my loving boy—and farewell for this time. WALT.

X

Brooklyn, September 15, 1870. DEAR PETE. Your letters of 10th and 12th have come safe, and are welcome

— dear son, I see that you are hard at work and appear to be in lively spirits — I am glad to hear you practice with the arithmetic — I wish you to try and do a little with it every day — practice makes perfect — you will see how soon and how clear it will all come to you — If you have the Geography or Atlas, look into that a little too — one needs to have an idea of the world too. I am concerned to hear of the death of Amos Dye — poor Amos — he was one of the first (I don't know but the very first) of the railroad men there I got acquainted with, and rode with — Pete if there is any further subscription for Mrs. Dye, I authorize you to put me down for $5. I will either send the money, or give it to her when I return. I shall return in about three weeks. I am now in the eighth week of my furlough — it is seven weeks last Tuesday night since we parted there at the corner of 7th Street. Well Pete, dear loving boy, I must now close for to-day. WALT. *Late Friday afternoon, September 16.* DEAR SON. I have time to add only a few words, in order to put it in the mail this evening. — I am working a while every day at my printing yet — but I go around considerable — still go out in the bay — and enjoy myself among my friends here — and in riding around, etc. — The weather is very fine, both days and nights — I don't know whether I told you how I stand now about the war — suffice it to say, that as things have gone on, and as the case stands, I find myself now far more for the *French* than I ever was for the Prussians — Then I propose to take my first drink with you when I return, in celebration of the pegging out of the Pope and all his gang of Cardinals and Priests — and entry of Victor Emanuel into Rome, and making it the capital of the great independent Italian nation. Good bye till next time, darling boy. WALT.

XI

Brooklyn, Friday, September 23 [1870]. DEAR PETE. Your letter of last Sunday and Monday came safe — was glad to see you so cheerful and feeling well, as seemed plain by the tone of the letter. All goes right with me. I am feeling well, and business matters move along as favorably as could be expected, taking all things in consideration. The weather is elegant — we had rain here too last Saturday and Sunday — and since then it has been clear and bright — I am out dashing around every day — fetch up home every night somewhere between 10 and 1 o'clock, quite tired. The river and bay get more and more beautiful, under these splendid September skies, the green waves and white foam relieved by the white sails of the crowds of ships and sail craft — for the shipping interest is brisker this fall than it has been for twelve years. Say to Harry Hurt, Mr. Shedd, Pensey and George Bell, Baley Murdock, George Smith. Dr. and Wash Milburn, or any of the railroad boys, or other friends that may inquire after me, that I send them my best respects — not forgetting my friends Mr. and Mrs.

Nash — also Father Boyle — (By the bye, Pete, I have taken a great fearful drink of whiskey, in honor of the news that arrived night before last of Victor Emanuel entering Rome — I couldn't wait.) Later — afternoon — It is now between 3 and 4 — I have been pitching in heavy to a great dish of stewed beef and onions mother cooked for dinner — and shall presently cross over to New York and mail this letter — shall probably go to some amusement with a friend this evening — most likely Buckley's Serenaders. — Pete, dear son, I hope this will find you all right, and everything lovely — It will not be long now before I shall be back — till then, take care of yourself, my loving son. WALT.

XII

Brooklyn, Friday afternoon, September 29 [1870].
DEAR SON. I am sitting here in my room, having just eat a hearty dinner with my mammy, (who has this month entered on her 76th year, but to my eyes looks young and handsome yet). — It is a dark and cloudy day and the rain is just now pouring down in torrents. It is a great disappointment to many, as Farragut's * funeral celebration was to come off to-day, and all the military, and departments here, and hundreds of societies, orders, schools, etc. had prepared to turn out — and most of them did

* David Glasgow Farragut, the celebrated American admiral, b. in Tenn. 5 July 1801, d. Portsmouth, N. H., 14 Aug. '70.

turn out this forenoon, only to get soaked with rain, and covered with mud — I saw one crack battalion, all so spruce and handsome, with white pants, and silver gray coats, and everything so bright and trim when they marched down — and an hour and a half afterwards, they looked like draggled roosters that had been pumped on — we have had weeks and weeks of the very finest weather up to early this morning and now it is the worst kind to be out in. Still we want rain so very much, one don't feel to complain. Pete, I received your last letter, the 26th — it was a good long, lively letter, and welcome — you write about the Signal Corps — Allen deserves credit for persevering and studying — and I hope he will do well — and think he will too — for he is sober, and tries to get ahead — anyhow he is a young man I like — Thornett is a very intelligent manly fellow, cute, plucky, etc.— he has one fault, and a bad one — that is he will drink, and spree it — which spoils all — True it is none of my business, but I feel that it would be perhaps the making of him, if he would give it up, and find his pleasure in some other way — Pete, should you see Allen again, give him my love — and the same for Thornett also. Did you mean for me to write what I think of your joining the Signal Corps? But are you proficient enough in studies?— I heartily advise you to peg away at the arithmetic — do something at it every day — arithmetic is the foundation of all such things (just as a good stone wall is the foundation for a house)— become a good arithmetician first of all — and you *surely will, if you keep pegging away a little every day* — how much leisure you have after all, that might be used for study — I don't mean all your leisure, but say one hour out of every three — then keep looking over the Geography — when I come back I will bring a little pocket Dictionary — with 15 minutes writing every day, and correcting by the dictionary I would warrant you becoming a correct speller and real handsome writer in a year or less — and when one is a fair arithmetician and spells and writes finely so many things are open to him. As things stand at present I expect to be back by or before next Sunday. WALT.

BEHOLD this swarthy face, these gray eyes,
This beard, the white wool unclipt upon my neck,
My brown hands and the silent manner of me without charm;
Yet comes one a Manhattanese and ever at parting kisses me
       lightly on the lip with robust love,
And I on the crossing of the street or on the ship's deck give a
       kiss in return,
We observe that salute of American comrades land and sea,
We are those two natural and nonchalant persons.
Leaves of Grass (Ed'n 1891), p. 105.

LETTERS OF 1871

I

BROOKLYN, *June* 21, 1871. DEAR PETE. I arrived home last night between 11 and 12 all safe and sound — found mother up waiting for me — It was dark and stormy, as rain had set in about 9 — had quite a pleasant journey — took a chair in the reserved seat car, 50 cents extra — plenty of room and a very easy riding car — thought while I was sitting up here now in my room waiting for dinner I would write a line to boy Pete. *Thursday forenoon.* The weather is very fine now here — plenty cool enough — I went over to New York yesterday afternoon and evening — took a ride up and down Broadway — am now laying off and taking it easy in my room — find it very pleasant here — fall just as natural into habits of doing nothing — lie on the sofa and read the papers — come up punctually to my meals — sleep a great deal — and take everything very quietly. *Friday* — Pete, I will finish this scribbling letter, and send it off so you will get it for Sunday — I am feeling well and enjoying myself doing nothing, spending a great deal of time with my mother, and going out a few hours every day on the river or over to New York — I hope you are feeling all right, and that everything is lovely — I believe that is all this

time — Love to you, dear son, and you must keep good heart through all the tribulations and botheration not only of railroading but life generally. I find tha Foster the "Car assassin" is an old driver and conducto that I knew quite well — he was a very good man, ver respectable, only a fool when drunk — it is the sadde case I know. He has three fine children — the public down upon him savage — and I suppose no hope for hir
WALT.

II

Brooklyn, July 7, 1871. DEAR PETE. Well here I a still, pretty much the same thing, doing nothing an taking things easy. By your letter I see that you to are jogging along about the same, on your car, with a occasional let up. Often in my jaunts around the Cit or on the bay, I wish you were with me, as you woul enjoy it much. I have seen Mr. Hart, formerly of th *Chronicle* — he is about the same in appearance a formerly. Pete, I will not write much this time, as I a feeling somewhat dull and stupid this forenoon. W had a fine shower last night, and there is some breeze - but it is pretty warm and oppressive — Pete, here is loving kiss for you, dear son, and much, much love fo you, as ever, from your affectionate comrade and fathe
WALT.

III

Brooklyn, Friday July 14 [1871.] DEAR PETE. It pretty much the same with me, as when I wrote m former letters — still home here with my mother, not busy at anything particular but taking a good deal of comfort— It has been very hot here, but one stands it better here than in Washington, on account perhaps of the sea-air — I am still feeling well, and am out around every day. There was quite a brush in N. Y. on Wednesday — the Irish lower orders, Catholic, had determined that the Orange parade, Protestant, should be put down— mob fired and threw stones — military fired on mob — between 30 and 40 killed, over a hundred wounded—but you have seen all about it in papers — it was all up in a distant part of the City, three miles from Wall street — five sixths of the City went on with its business just the same as any other day — I saw a big squad of prisoners carried along under guard — they reminded me of the squads of rebel prisoners brought in Washington, six years ago. The New York police looked and behaved splendidly — no fuss, few words, but *action* — great, brown, bearded, able, American looking fellows, (Irish stock, though, many of them) — I had great pleasure in looking on them — something new, to me, it quite set me up to see such chaps, all dusty and worn, looked like veterans — Pete, dear son, I received your two letters, and was glad to get them.— Mother has been quite sick, and I have been sort of nurse, as she is here alone, none of my sisters being home at present — she is much better this morning, under my doctoring. Pete, I see by your letters that everything goes on right with you on the

CALAMUS

road — give my best regards to my friends among the drivers and conductors. Dear son, I shall now soon be coming back, and we will be together again, as my leave is up on the 22nd,— I am now going to take a bath and dress myself to go over to New York. Love to you, my dearest boy, and good bye for this time. WALT.

IV

[*Sunday, 16 July, 1871.*] *By the sea-shore, Coney Island, Sunday 3 p. m.* DEAR PETE. I will write you a few lines as I sit here, on a clump of sand by the sea shore — having some paper in my haversack, and an hour or two yet before I start back. Pete, I wish you were with me the few hours past — I have just had a splendid swim and souse in the surf — the waves are slowly rolling in, with hoarse roar that is music to my ears — the breeze blows pretty brisk from southwest, and the sun is partially clouded — from where I sit I look out on the bay and down the Narrows, vessels sailing in every direction in the distance — a great big black long ocean steamship streaking it up toward New York — and the lines of hills and mountains, far, far away on the Jersey coast, a little veiled with blue vapor — here around me, as I sit it is nothing but barren sand — but I don't know how long I could sit here, to that soothing rumbling murmuring of the waves — and then the salt breeze. *Friday, July* [21]. DEAR SON. I wrote the preceding nearly a week ago, intending to finish and send it then— Nothing very new or special with me— Mother has been quite unwell, gets better, then worse again —I have applied for a few days' further leave— The weather here remains nearly perfect— we have had but three or four uncomfortably hot days the past five weeks — every day a fine breeze smelling of the sea. Pete, if you are still working, and all is going on smooth, you can send me that $50.— you might get Mr. Milburn to send it to me by Post Office Order — give it to him with this envelope, and ask him to go to P. O. and send a P. O. Order to me— it will save you the trouble — But Pete, dear boy, if anything has turned up in meantime, you needn't send it, as I can get along otherwise— I am doing well, both in health and *business prospects* here— my book is doing first rate— so everything is lovely and the goose hangs high — Your loving comrade and father. WALT.

V

Brooklyn, Monday forenoon, July 24 [1871]. DEAR PETE. I received the $50 to-day all right, and a real help to me — I have money but I cannot have the use of it just now — so this comes first rate.— I spent yesterday down on the sea-shore, was all by myself, had a splendid good day, took my dinner with me— went down in the boat twelve miles in the morning, and back in a big open horse car toward evening through the fields and woods — very pleasant indeed — staid a long while in the water

CALAMUS

— weather perfect — Mother is better to-day — she has been pretty sick, with several ups and downs — I am as well as a fellow can be — eat and sleep tremendous — shall stay here a week or so longer — shall be back first part of next week if nothing happens — Well Pete, I believe that is all this morning — Good bye, my darling son, and a long, long kiss from your loving father. WALT.

VI

Brooklyn, July 28 [1871, *Friday*]. DEAR SON. I shall return on Monday next, in the 12.30 train from Jersey City — (the train I usually come in). Pete, I have received your letter of 26th. Mother seems to-day full as well as usual — I continue all right — I have been on to New Haven, about 75 miles from here — a former friend of mine is in a dying condition there from consumption, and expressed such a strong desire to see me, that I went on I thought he would die while I was there — he was al wasted to a skeleton, faculties good, but voice only a low whisper — I returned last night, after midnight. — Well bub, my time here is short — I have had a good quie visit — the best in some respects yet — and I feel satisfiec — My darling son, we will very soon be together again your loving comrade, WALT.

LETTERS OF 1872

I

BROOKLYN, 107 *North Portland Av., Feb.* 16, 1872. DEAR PETE. Dear, dear son. We are having a very cold spell here, the severest of the winter — freezes up the pipes through the house, and burst them yesterday, causing great trouble — I too have got a bad cold, my head all stopped. I came through all right last Saturday, on time — quite a pleasant trip — Mother is very well, full as well as usual — I am having quiet good times, home with mother — stay in the house more than usual on account of the bitter cold (but go out two or three hours during the day). I will only write this very short letter to you this time, but send you my love, my darling son — I think about you every day, dear son — will write more soon — here is a kiss for you, dear loving son. WALT. Pete, I am making out a poor scraggy letter to you this time — I feel pretty well, but don't seem to feel like writing — Good bye for to-day, my loving boy. Your true Father and comrade always.

II

Brooklyn, Friday noon, Feb. 23 [1872]. DEAR SON. Your letter received this morning speaks of the mild

CALAMUS

weather there — but it has been and remains very cold here — so much so that I don't go around half as much as I would like. My cold hangs on, though not so bad as at first. The state of the weather, and my cold, etc., have rather blocked me from having my usual enjoyment here, so far — but I expect to make up for it by and by. Dear son, I see you are off* — I take it by your letter that you are feeling well in health, and having as good a time as the law allows — I wish we could be together there, some of these moonlight nights — but here it is too cold for comfort — (the water pipes here froze again last night, causing trouble) — I go out a couple of hours middle of the day, but keep in nights — I have got the new edition of my book under way — and it will be satisfactory I think — It will be in one volume, and will make a better appearance than any of the former ones — Do you go up to the Debates in the Senate? — I see by the papers they are having high times — Senator Schurz appears to come out ahead of them all — he is a real good speaker — I enjoy the way he shakes them up, (very much like a first class terrier in a pit, with a lot of rats). Pete, I send you $10 enclosed, as you may need it — Should you want more, you write, as I have plenty — I am writing this up in my back room, home — have had a nice breakfast of hot potatoes and first-rate Oregon salmon, with the best coffee that's made — home-made

* *i. e.* off work.

bread and sweet butter — everything tip-top — get along well enough — you must try to do the same — so goodbye for this time, my own loving boy — WALT.

III

Brooklyn, Monday evening, March 4 [1872]. DEAR SON. I am sitting here in my room home, alone — it is snowing hard and heavy outside and cold and wintry as ever — there has not been one mild day here for the past three weeks — two thirds of the time spiteful and gusty wind and clouds of dust — and this with bitter cold — seems to me I have felt the cold more than for the last three winters — But I reckon I have said enough on this point. — Pete, I cannot write anything interesting to you as I do not go anywhere nor see anything new — I have attended to the bringing out the new edition of my book, but as the plates were all ready before, it is not much of a job — I am home every night (and half the days also). *Tuesday noon.* I am afraid this letter is not destined to be very cheering — I was attacked last night with sore throat, pretty bad — still I make out this morning to worry down a fair breakfast — the weather has been so infernal — last evening towards sundown, begun the spitefulest wind and cold I ever knew, great clouds suddenly come up, inky black, and all of a sudden snow fell so thick and fast, it was like a dense fog, — so thick the hard wind didn't dissipate it in the least — this lasted about half an

CALAMUS

hour, and was about the highest old weather exhibition ever witnessed — snow fell two inches thick in fifteen minutes. Dear Pete, how are you getting along? — how about Sailer and the R. R.? — I suppose slow and aggravating enough — by what you said in your last. Dear Pete, I don't think I shall stay here as long as I originally intended — I shall be back, by, or before, the end of this month — I am writing these lines home in the kitchen — mother is sitting in the rocking chair sewing something — and Eddy* is grinding some good coffee in a coffee mill it smells good — (I have retreated to the kitchen for the hot fire — here now I am not like I am in Washington — you would laugh to see me hovering over the fire) — My darling son you must keep a good heart — don't get discouraged — love to you, baby, I enclose $10. — and can send you whatever you want — WALT.

IV

Brooklyn, Thursday forenoon [*March* 7, 1892]. DEAR SON. Well, I am still here, Pete, kept in pretty close quarters by the weather — but it seems to be something of a let up this morning. There is nothing special to

---

* Edward Whitman, a younger brother who was imbecile. Walt Whitman always spoke of him as "crippled." He provided for Eddy during a large part of his (W. W's.) life and made provision for his maintenance in his will. But Eddy died in 1892 only a few weeks after W. W's. own death.

write about — but I thought I would send you a line this morning. I sent you a letter two days ago with $10. — (the second $10 I have sent) write me whether you received it all right. I hope you are not discouraged by the way things work on the road — It won't be very long now before I shall be back with you — Give my love to Mr. and Mrs. Nash — tell Wash Milburne I wish him success in the "graduate of pharmacy" line, and everything else — give him my love.— Pete, I believe that is all this time, dear baby, WALT. With a kiss from your loving father.

V

107 *North Portland Ave., Brooklyn, March* 15 [1872]. DEAR SON. I will just write you a line, as you may be looking for word from me Saturday. The weather has let up a little, but it is cold enough yet — I have been to the Italian Opera twice, heard Nilsson both times,—she is *very fine* — One night *Trovatore*, and one, *Robert*, with Brignoli — both good. I expect to return in about two weeks — I am writing this here in the kitchen, home,— I have deserted my own room this visit, as it is so cold even with a fire — Mother had a bad spell three days, commencing Sunday last — but is about as usual to-day and yesterday — We have splendid buckwheat cakes for breakfast — sometimes I fry them myself — I wish you could just be here and eat breakfast — I think my mammy makes the best coffee in the world, and buck-

CALAMUS

wheats ditto — mince-pies ditto.— My new edition* looks best yet — it is from the same plates as the last only in one Volume bound handsomely in green cloth — my books are beginning to do pretty well — I send you the publisher's slip.— Well, Pete, I believe that is all this time. Remember me to any of the boys on the road that may inquire for me — also Adrian Jones, that works in the theatre — it is now after ten, Friday forenoon, clear, cold, and windy — and I am going over to New York to have a lot of my books sent to England by tomorrow's steamer. Dear son, I send my best love, as always. We will soon be together again, dear son. WALT.

VI

Brooklyn, Friday forenoon, March 22 [1872]. DEAR PETE, I received your letter yesterday. Pete, you must be quite steady at work, and no time to spare. Well perhaps it is just as satisfactory considering all things The cold weather has just kept on here, as before — cold enough all the time — and then a spell of damned bitter stinging cold every now and then extra — not one single mild warm day since I have been home — six weeks — I am middling well, go out some every day, but not much — Best thing is my *eating* and *sleeping* — I fall back or them altogether — I sleep splendid, have a good bed plenty of cover — get up pretty early though and make

* *i. e.*, the '72 edn. of the "Leaves." The '71 edn. was issued in pale green *paper* covers — the '72 in dark green cloth.

the fire, and set things agoing, before mother comes out
— she has had some bad times with rheumatism, etc. —
one hand and arm quite disabled — still she is very
cheerful, looks well in the face, and does more work
cooking, etc., than most young women — We have grand
breakfasts, buckwheat cakes, coffee, etc., eggs, etc. —
just wish you could come in mornings and partake. We
two * always breakfast together, and it is first rate — So
you see I fall back upon sleeping and eating, (as I said)
— Should be glad to see Parker Milburn — hope he
will call to-day — I send you a paper by mail.— Well,
Pete, I believe that is all, this time. Good bye, my
darling son — So the *new shirts* turn out a success do
they? I have a great mind to be jealous — Give my
love to Wash Milburn, Adrian Jones, and all the R. R.
boys. Your loving old WALT.

VII

Brooklyn, Friday afternoon [*March* 29, 1872.] DEAR
BOY PETE. I have received your letter, and the paper
with the account of Mr. Huntington's death — it seems a
sudden and sorrowful thing — Pete, I shall continue here
another week — I see you are working [it] appears quite
steady — I continue pretty well — Mother is middling —
This last two days the weather has been real pleasant —
I have been out most of the time — It is now between 4
and 5 — I am writing this up in my room, home — am

* *i. e.* his mother and himself.

CALAMUS

going out, and over to New York this evening — Nothing special to write about — Pete, my darling boy, I have been writing some long letters on business, etc. — and feel very little like writing (so I will just dry up for this occasion), here is a good buss to you dear son from you loving father always.

VIII

Brooklyn, Friday forenoon, April 5 [1872]. DEAR SON I expect to be back in Washington next week — some where in the middle of the week.— I am well— Mother is pretty well — I received your letter three days since — Pete, things must be going on about the same as ever — As I write it is pleasant weather, and I am going out to get the good of it — Pete, take care of yourself till I see you, dear boy. WALT.

IX

Brooklyn, 107 *North Portland Ave., June* 14 [1872] DEAR SON. I got home all right Saturday night — and have been having quite a good time. There is nothing very new — Mother is well as usual. I shall print my College poem* in a small book — it will be small — and

* The poem referred to was read by W. W. at "Commencement, Dartmouth College, N. H., 26 June, '72, on invitation of the United Literary Societies. It was afterwards printed in a small volume which was called by the name of this poem: *As a Strong Bird o Pinions Free and other Poems. Washington, D.C. 1872.* In th current *Leaves* (1891-2) it will be found, p. 346, under the heading "Thou Mother with thy Equal Brood."

is intended as the beginning of a larger one—I am having it set up at the printing office—will send you one in ten or twelve days. Pete, how are you getting along?— I suppose on 14 the same as when I was there—I see by the papers that the head men have mostly migrated from Washington, and that it is said to be hot and dull enough there.—Do you see anything of Mr. Tasistro?*— I received the letter he sent to the office for me—I am writing this in the house in Portland Av.—we are having a showery afternoon—Good bye, my darling boy—and I will try to write again soon (and a more interesting letter)—WALT.

X

Brooklyn, June 18, 1872. DEAR PETE. I am having a better time here than I had my last visit. The weather is very pleasant—pretty hot during the middle of the day, but mornings and nights perfect—No moonlight walks out beyond Uniontown here—but I go on the river and cross to and fro in the pilot house. Last night was beautiful—Saturday I spent at Coney Island—went in swimming—Mother is only middling—has some pretty bad spells with rheumatism—will break up here,

* Count Michael Tasistro, of French-Irish parentage, came originally to this country with a hunting party of French noblemen. He remained here permanently and, becoming poor, supported himself by teaching French and by literary work. He died while engaged in the translation of the Comte de Paris' *History of the Civil War.*

CALAMUS

and go with my brother George to Camden, N. J., in September. I suppose you got a letter from me las Saturday, as I wrote you the day before. Pete, dea son, if you should want any of your money send m word. It is either $120 or $130 (I am not sure — bu I have a memorandum in my desk at Washington) — am feeling real well, and I hope you are too, my loving boy. WALT.

XI

Hanover, N. H., Thursday, June 27 [1872]. DEAI SON. I will write you just a line to show you I am her away north, and alive and kicking. I delivered m poem here before the College yesterday. All went of very well. — (It is rather provoking — after feeling un usually well this whole summer, — since Sunday last have been about half sick and am so yet, by spells.) am to go to Vermont for a couple of days, and then bacl to Brooklyn. — Pete I received your letter, that you ha been taken off — write to me Saturday 30th, or Sunda — direct to usual address 107 Portland Ave., Brooklyn I will send you the little book with my poem, (an others) when I get back to Brooklyn. Pete, did m poem appear in the Washington papers — I suppos Thursday or Friday — *Chronicle* or *Patriot* ? If so sen me one — (or one of each). — It is a curious scen here, as I write, a beautiful old New England village 150 years old, large houses and gardens, great elms plenty of hills — every thing comfortable, but very Yankee — *not an African to be seen all day* — not a grain of dust — not a car to be seen or heard — green grass everywhere — no smell of coal tar. — As I write a party are playing base ball on a large green in front of the house — the weather suits me first rate — cloudy but no rain. Your loving WALT.

XII

Brooklyn, June 30 [1872]. DEAR BOY. I received your letter of Tuesday last, and was glad to hear everything was going on all right. I am well, and still enjoying myself in a quiet way — I have been home every evening since I come — but out quite a good deal in the day — the weather is splendid here — plenty cool enough. This has got to be a great place for boating — all the rich men have their yachts, and most every young man belongs to a boat or yacht club — sometimes of a pleasant day, especially Sunday, you will see them out all over up and down the bay in swarms — the yachts look beautiful enough, with white sails and many with white hulls and their long pennants flying — it is a new thing to see them so plenty. 11 *o'clock, Friday forenoon.* Pete, I am sitting in my room, home, finishing this — have just had a bath, and dressed myself to go over to New York, partly on business — shall go down and put this in the P. O. here — shall walk down, as it is a very pleasant forenoon. — When you write tell me if you have read

CALAMUS

Charles Reade's novel of "Foul Play"—if not, I have one here I will send you—Dear son, I believe that is all this time—I send my love, dear son, and a good loving kiss—I think of you every day—Give my best regards to all enquiring friends, and inform them I expect to be back in about three weeks—Good bye, my darling boy, —from your comrade and father. WALT.

XIII

Brooklyn, July 12 [1872]. DEAR SON PETE. I have been sick—but am feeling better now, and soon expect to be all right. Mother too is unwell. I expect to remain here ten or twelve days longer. Pete, I will only write a short letter this time—Love to you, dear son. WALT.

XIV

New York, Friday afternoon, July 19 [1872]. DEAR BOY PETE. I received your letter yesterday—nothing very new with me—am better than I was when I wrote you before—shall return to Washington next week, somewhere about the middle of the week. Pete, you must try to keep good heart—Perhaps this will find you at work again—if not, you must keep up a cheerful heart all the same. I have just been spending a couple of hours with Joaquin Miller—I like him real well. $10. enclosed. WALT.

LETTERS OF 1873

I

[1873]. DEAR PETE. I have been very unwell—but am better again—at least at the present moment. I am stopping at Mr. Ashton's, 1202 K St. next door to the southwest corner of K and 12th*— come up and see me—I wrote you a line two days ago, to Milburn's— Did you not get it? WALT.†

II

Camden,‡ *May* 31. [1873]. I expect to return Monday,§ June 2 between half-past 5 and 6, but probably too late to see you that evening. Come up Tuesday. I am about the same as to my sickness—no worse. WALT.

* In Washington.

† This note was probably written between 1st and 26th Jan. '73. Between it and the next letter in this volume intervene *Letters in Sickness* (26 Jan. to 16 May, '73) written to his mother and printed in *In Re Walt Whitman*, pp. 73-92.

‡ Walt Whitman left Washington the 20th May—pretty sick— left arm and leg paralyzed—and for a time lived with his brother George in Camden, N. J.

§ He almost certainly did not return to Washington as intended —see—infra—letter of 28 Aug. '73.

CALAMUS

III

322 *Stevens St., Camden, N. J. Wednesday forenoon
June* 18 [1873]. DEAR PETE. It has been a good move
of me coming here, as I am pleasantly situated, have two
rooms on 2nd floor, with north and south windows, so
can have the breeze through—I can have what I wish in
the grub line, have plenty of good strawberries—and my
brother and sister are very kind—It is very quiet, and
I feel like going in for getting well—There is not much
change so far—but I feel comparatively comfortable since
I have been here—and better satisfied—My brother is
full of work (inspecting pipe manufactured here at the
foundries for water works and sewers in northern cities
—he is in splendid health—a great stout fellow—weighs
more than I do—he is building a handsome new house
here, to be done latter part of August. *Thursday* 19th
Nothing very new—I have had some bad feeling in the
head yesterday afternoon and this morning—but it will
pass over no doubt—It is warm weather here, days, but
pleasant nights so far—Pete, when you get the *Star* save
it and send to me—you can send two in a wrapper with
a one cent stamp. (I enclose some, for fear you haven't
any). *Friday* 20th. Pretty hot weather here and need
rain badly—I am about the same—feel pretty well for
a while, and then have a bad spell—have distress in the
head at times, but keep up a good heart—or at any rate
try to.—Give my respects to all enquiring friends—to

them I expect to return to Washington in about a couple of months — tell me who you meet, and every little thing, and who asks about me, etc., as it will interest me. — I have made a raise of some new summer clothes, real nice — thin black pants and vest, a blue flannel suit, and some white vests. — Love to Wash Milburn — let him read this letter if he wishes — Write how you are getting along — Good bye dear son. WALT.

IV

[*Camden,*] *Thursday evening, June* 26 [1873]. DEAR PETE. I received your note to-day. I send you a note I have written to Mr. Edmunds, — first take it to Mr. Noyes, (to whom it is enveloped,) and get an additional line I have requested from him — and then, if you conclude to try for the carrier's place, — go up and take it yourself to Mr. Edmunds. I must tell you another thing. I have written (wrote yesterday) a short note to Mr. Dubarry, your superintendent, asking him if you couldn't be better placed when the changes of the Baltimore connection are made. It may not amount to anything but I took a notion to write it. Pete, I am not having a very good time — my head troubles me — yesterday was as bad as ever — as far from well as ever — to-day I am a little easier, and have been out a few steps. But I keep up a good heart, dear son — and you must too. WALT. If you conclude not to try for the carrier's berth, let the letters go.

CALAMUS

V

322 *Stevens St., Camden, N. J., Monday,* [*July*] ; [1873]. DEAR SON. I am only able to write the same old story — since I last wrote, I have had some pretty bad spells — suffered at intervals all last week, and yesterday, with the strange and painful distress in the head, I have had so much of — But I feel better to-day - Every time I feel better, I find myself much encouraged — I still stick here, as I don't dare to trust myself in a strange place, if I can help it. I received your letter telling me you was too late to get any chance for the letter carrier's position — and about Mr. Noyes' friendliness — Are things just the same, as far as you and your crew are concerned? — I think about you every night — I reproach myself that I did not fly around when I was well, and in Washington, to find some better employment for you — now I am here, crippled, laid up for God knows how long, unable to help myself, or my dear boy — I do not miss anything of Washington here, but *your visits* — if I could only have a daily visit here such as I had there — I go out very little here — there is not much convenience here, for me to go out — one car line passing about two squares off, consists of four cars, running semi-occasionally — and another line, about 3½ squares the other way, has I believe 6 or 7 cars — I get out and take a ride in them sometimes — my best jaunt is going in them to the ferry, and crossing on the boat to Phila

delphia, to and fro, several times — But a great portion of the time I do not feel able to go out alone — fortunately I do not have any dizzy spells, nor any symptoms of them, so far, — so I am not worried about that when I am out — As I write this it is a very pleasant cool afternoon and I am sitting here by the window in a big easy chair. Pete, I hope this will find you feeling well, and in good spirits. — Write me a good long letter and tell me everything — it will do you good — how does the new time go on the road, since Baltimore Tunnel connection — how about Washington — Tasistro — every body. Get a good sheet of paper, and sit down in the Park with your lead pencil — I send you an envelope — also some one cent stamps. — Love to you, dear boy — keep up a good heart — I do yet — though it is a long and hard pull sometimes with me lately. WALT.

VI

Camden, Tuesday afternoon, July 15 [1873]. DEAR PETE. There is nothing new or different with me — I am no better in any respect, don't know what is going to come out of it all — We are having pretty hot weather here just now, but it does not affect me much — it is no near as oppressive here as the Washington heat — I received your letter, my dear son — with the paper — I will write more to-morrow. *Wednesday afternoon.* Pete, I have little to write to you about, as I remain anchored here in the house nearly all the time. As I write I am sitting in my mother's former room, in her old armchair.— Spend a great deal of my time here, as I haven't felt like going out lately — half a block tires me. Pete, my darling son, I still think I shall weather it but time only can show — Mother's death is on my mind yet,* time does not lift the cloud from me at all — I want much to get to the sea-shore, either Long Island or the Jersey coast, and shall make a start if I get strong enough — It is not so hot here to-day. So long, my darling boy. WALT.

VII

Camden, Thursday noon, July 24, 1873. DEAR SON PETE:— It is still the same old story with me — the best I can say is that I don't seem to get worse, even if I don't get better. Your letter came, and the *Star*, with the item about Tasistro. It must be very hot there in Washington, but you stand it better than most any one I know. I too never used to think anything of heat or cold, from 20 to 50 — but last summer I felt the heat severely, for the first time. Pete, as I have told you several times, I still think I shall get over this, and we will be together again and have some good times — but for all that it is best for you to be prepared for something different — my strength can't stand the pull forever, and if continued must sooner or later give out —

* Mrs. Whitman died May 23, 1873.

LETTERS OF 1873

Now Pete, don't begin to worry boy, or cry about me, for you haven't lost me yet, and I really don't think it is likely yet — but I thought it best to give a word of caution, if such a thing should be — I am quite comfortable here and have everything I want — I went out at ½ past 5 yesterday afternoon, and rode in the cars here to the ferry, and crossed the Delaware from Camden to Philadelphia four or five times — very pleasant. To-day is burning hot, but I am feeling as well as usual. *Friday 25th, 4 o'clock.* Pretty hot again to-day here, but not so oppressive to bear as in Washington — I am feeling about as usual to-day — shall try to get out a few steps after I send this — Good bye for this time, dear loving son. WALT.

VIII

Pete you must read this over Sunday, as a ten minutes' talk like, about all sorts of odds and ends.

Camden, Friday afternoon, Aug. 1 [1873]. DEAR SON. Your letter is received to-day, and enclosed I send you $20. — I want you to write soon — as I shall want to know if it reached you safe. I am feeling relieved of the worst distress in the head now for the last two days — had it straight along bad enough the first three days in the week — but yesterday and to-day it has mostly let up — have been out to-day, and over to Philadelphia — it is hard work, especially as I have no one to go with me

CALAMUS

— but I put a bold face on, *and my best foot foremost* — I
Wash Milburn there in the store? or has he gone on h
vacation in the country?—answer me in your next—
think of writing a few lines to him— Hot weather her
but I don't suffer much from it—though I think it is ba
for me, and I hope much more from the cool season, if
get through this— Pete, I too see quite a good deal (
Railroad, and hear more— some 70 rods off is the gre:
depot of the Camden and Amboy, bells and whistles an
trains rumbling continually, night and day, and lots (
R. R. men living near, around here — if I only felt just
little better I should get acquainted with many of the mei
which I could very easily do if I would. I should muc
like to go on the trips so handy and cheap, right as yc
might from my door, to Cape May, or to Long Brancl
etc., to say nothing of the numerous fine jaunts fro:
Philadelphia G. R. R., or up or down the Delaware b
Steamboat — If you was only here to convoy me — but
suppose no one is to have *every thing* wanting — (Pet
dear son, there was $89. coming to you, of the money yc
put in my charge, and now there will be $69. yet due yc
from me— your own soap) — As I write it is 4½ o'cloc
Friday afternoon — I am sitting here alone, in the 2r
story front room — every thing quiet here — I receive
the other letter, and *Sunday Chronicle* — When you writ
tell me who you see, and everything.— I like such lette
far better than the formal ones some send me — I had
visit from a good, kind-hearted, rather queer old fello

named Ingram, from Philadelphia — he said he see* in the Philadelphia paper I was laid up very sick in Camden — so he came over and hunted for hours through the hot sun, found me at last — he evidently had thought I was keeled up, and hard up, and he came to offer help — he has been a great traveler, is English by birth — I found him good company, and was glad to see him — he has been twice — so you see there are good souls left — Pete, when you see Judge Fisher tell him I shall yet be back all right one of these days, and in the mean time tell him I send him my love — also my love to Mr. and Mrs. Nash the next time you go there — So good bye for the present, my darling son, and you must keep good heart, for I do, though it is pretty glum around and over me sometimes. WALT.

IX

Camden, August 22 [1873]. DEAR SON. I received your letter of last Saturday and Sunday — and was interested in reading all the particulars you wrote about the R. R. etc., and the young man, your friend the fireman — poor fellow, it was indeed a sad fate — There has been great washing away and trouble with R. R. tracks hereabout too — for myself I never remember an August with so much rain — Write to me whether your road has repaired damages, and is running through again — also everything you think of and see about people and Wash-

* So in MSS.

CALAMUS

ington, etc., that would interest me — as I live a very
quiet life here. I am still about the same as when I las
wrote — am no worse and not much better — though
perceive my general strength is at least as good as any
time since I have been sick — my head still troubles me
with pain and distress a good deal of the time — I hobble
out a little every day when not prevented by the rain —
and console myself with thinking that everything with
me might be a great deal worse — I can put up with al
but the death of my mother — that is my great sorrow
that sticks — affects me just as much now, or more, than
at the time. Have you seen Mr. Eldridge since hi
return to Washington? — Have you seen anything of Mr
O'Connor? — (You know he is now Chief Clerk of the
Light House Board) — You must have had a sweet time
with Dr. Duncan and Dr. Blake, (though I must confes
I rather like the latter, — I suspect he has some real good
points) — sometimes when one has plenty of time, I think
it very good, for a change, to let such fellows buzz you to
their heart's content, when you fall in with them — think
of them as acting a part for your amusement — how wel
they do it — if they could only do it on the stage, it would
make their fortune — So Mr. Tasistro still lives — h
deserves great credit for his perseverance and vitality —
I hope he will come to the top of the heap yet — I cut ou
the piece below from a Philadelphia paper, thinking
might interest you — As I sit here in my arm chair, fin
ishing this, it is 3 o'clock Friday afternoon, it clouds u

again as if for rain, we had a shower last night — it was quite cool, but has been pretty warm here for two days, and is now — I am feeling as if I would and should come out all right yet — had a nice dinner — Pete, dear son, send me the *Sunday Herald* Aug. 24. — don't forget — So long, dear son. WALT.

X

Camden, Thursday evening, [Aug. 28, 1873]. PETE, DEAR SON. I am not sinking nor getting worse — I have had some very bad times, and have some pretty bad ones yet, mostly with my head — and my leg is about as useless as ever — still I am decidedly no worse, and I think now I am even *getting better* — it is slow and with great alternations — but I have the feeling of getting more strength, and easier in the head — something like what I was before Mother's death — I cannot be reconciled to that yet — it is the great cloud of my life — nothing that ever happened before has had such an effect on me — but I shall get well, yet, dear son, probably, (of course not certainly) and be back in Washington this fall, and we will be together again. I think I am now about as I was the day you came down to Baltimore Depot with me — 20th May, I think. *Friday after dinner.* I have thought of you the nights of this week, the heaviest rains here almost ever known, great trouble and loss to railroads — was you in any tight spot? — that described in your last made me feel a little nervous — That was a fearful disaster of the Wawasset — sad beyond description — So Tasistro is around yet — The *Chronicle* came — Mr. Eldridge has returned to Washington from his month's leave — he stopped here and paid me a 3 or 4 hour's visit — John Burroughs has an article in the Sept. number of *Scribner's Magazine*, just out, in which I am extracted from — Pete, it is now towards 3, and I am going to try to get down to the Ferry boat, and cross to Philadelphia — so you see I am not altogether disabled — but it is awful tough work — when the weather is cooler, (which will be soon) I shall be better off in Washington, as it is very lonesome to me here, and no one to convoy me — I shall return there — I want to get a couple of unfurnished rooms, or top floor, somewhere on or near the car route — Pete, if you see Charley Toner give him my love, and ask him to give you his address to send me — He works in the Printing Bureau (M'Cartee's) Treasury Goodbye, my dear loving boy. WALT.

XI

Camden, Friday noon, Sept. 5 [1873]. DEAR BOY PETE Your letter, with cheering wishes and prophecies, came last Tuesday, God bless you, boy,— for all such things help much — I had a bad spell this morning have something of the kind pretty often — still it seems certain I am improving, generally,— and that my general strength is better, I am not near as bad as I was five weeks ago — have some hours in which I feel quite like myself again — keep up good heart nearly all the time — and you must too, dear son. So I see Beau Hickman * has died of a stroke of paralysis — in the paper this morning I see a piece about his body being resurrected from Potter's field. Pete, I see a collision of some trains on the B. & P. road reported in the tunnel at Baltimore yesterday morning early in which a brakeman named Hankinson was instantly killed — I was over to Philadelphia yesterday — there is a large reading room, the Mercantile Library, 10th St. where I go occasionally — it is quite handy — they have all the papers from everywhere — have the *Washington Chronicle, Capital*, etc. Then I took a ride in the Market St. cars, and was caught in a violent rain at ½ past 7 coming home — the moment I got home it stopt, and cleared off a beautiful moonlit night. It is clear and pretty hot here to-day — I am sitting here in the front room, in the same big old mahogany chair I gave mother 20 years ago, by the open window writing this — I am feeling better since breakfast. Pete, the papers you sent came last Monday all right — I have received a letter from Chas. Eldridge — and another from Walter Godey, the young man who is working for

---

* " Beau " Hickman was a familiar character in Washington, a decayed dandy, who made periodical visits through the Capitol and the Departments, picking up a living from the contributions of congressmen and government officials, many of whom were his regular patrons.

me as my substitute in the office — all was going on well
in the office — I send a couple of papers to-day — nothing particular — send the *Herald*. Did I tell you that a
doctor I have talked with here says my real disease is
*the brain not being properly furnished and nourished with
blood?* —(it is a disease the doctors call *cerebral anaemia*)
— the doctor says it has been long a coming, and will be
long a going — says I will get over it though — says the
paralysis comes from that, and that it (the paralysis) is
not very formidable — I am following Dr. Drinkard's
advice, taking no medicine, living very carefully. WALT.

XII

Camden, Friday afternoon, Sept. 12 [1873]. DEAR BOY
PETE. It is a very fine September day here — it must be
delightful down in Virginia — the sun shines just warm
enough and there is a slight haze, which makes it just
right — I have been out just a little but was glad to get
back — I am feeling tolerable, but my leg still gives out
in a few minutes' walk — I have had two or three quite
good spells this week, sufficient to arouse my hopes, but
am in a pretty bad way yet — however, I am not without
some pretty steady *small* expectations, if not great ones.
I am enough better to be perceptible, and to make me in
hopes of being better still —(but I have so many times
got a little better, only to fall back again as bad as ever,
or worse) — I have just had my dinner, nice beefsteak,

you feeling well, & in good
spirits — Write me a good
long letter, & tell me every
thing — it will do you good —
how does the new time go on
the road, since Baltimore tunnel Connection?
— how about Washington —
Cassitro — everybody? — get
a good sheet of paper, &
sit down in the Park, with
your lead pencil — I send you
an envelope — also some
one cent stamps ——

Love to you dear boy —
Keep up a good heart —
I do yet — though it is
a long & hard pull sometimes
with me lately.
                                Walt

potatoes, etc. My appetite still holds out — and my sister cooks very nice, gets me what I want. —Pete, your letter of Sept. 1, came safe — also the *Herald* and *Republican* — I send you Philadelphia papers. My brother Jeff has been on here this week from St. Louis — got in a car in St. Louis, 6 Saturday evening, week ago, took off his boots for easy shoes, and (sleeping, he says, very well and sound in his bed on the car,) had his meals regular and got in here at Philadelphia about 9 o'clock Monday morning, in the same car, (which went on to New York) — He is now out on a good yacht excursion, from N. Y. out in the sound and sea, for a week — quite a voyage — He only stopped here 3 or 4 hours — but is to return last of the month — both my brothers are stout and hearty, and full of business, and interested in it thoroughly — and doing well. I hear quite often from John Burroughs — he has bought a spot of land, right on the Hudson river, about 80 miles from N. Y. and is building himself a house there, right on a steep bank with the road on one side, and the river on the other (but sufficient space between) a 2 ½ story stone house — I have heard from Charley Towner — I got a very nice letter from him Thursday — he said you met him Tuesday and told him — A long while ago, I wanted to get a house in conjunction with Charley and his family — where I could have a couple of rooms, and they could see to them — and that was one thing I wanted to write to him about, to see if we could do it now — but he tells me his wife is quite sick — I quite pricked up my ears to read the short interview between Mr. Dubarry and you, and what he said about the *schedule*, etc. — I see you are a little nervous, Pete — and I don't wonder, nor blame you — Still the true point to attain is (like a good soldier, or officer), to keep on the alert, to do one's duty fully, without fail — and leave the rest to God Almighty. I was reading the paper here this morning, and I see a list of some new inventions said to work first rate, among the rest this* for car coupling — I wonder if there is anything in it — It is awful the way men are slaughtered of late years on the trains — there must be three or four hundred every year, take the country through — and the papers put 'em in in items of three or four lines, down somewhere out of the way — such a thing as the killing of that young man Harkinson, in the Baltimore tunnel, a grand magnificent young *man*, no doubt (while half the papers in the land have had long obituaries and notices of the death of that rotten old apple, Beau Hickman †). Well, son, I have made out quite a letter for you this time — My brother and I have been talking about the balloon splurge in New York - my brother is quite a balloonist, in his belief — believes that something will yet come of it — I see they advertise to go yet, perhaps this afternoon — but it is a wild under-

---

* Referring to a short newspaper article on " A New Car Coupler " which he pastes in his letter.

† See note on page 111.

taking — (perhaps an advertising humbug) anyhow. I shall still remain here for the present — everything seems to be going on smooth in the office at my desk, from what I hear from my substitute — He writes me now and then, does my work very well, and more work besides, — Dear Pete, I am much in hopes I shall be able to send some news before long about my improvement for good — and something definite about my coming back to Washington — So long, dear son — you must try to keep up a gay heart and let the world wag on as it may. WALT.

XIII

Camden, Friday afternoon, Sept. 19 [1873]. DEAR BOY PETE. Your letter came all right last Tuesday. I still keep the same — no worse, and no better. It is the same old story. I have a great deal of pain in my head yet — no let up. Dear son, I would like to write you a good long amusing letter — but I cannot to-day. We have had a rainy night and forenoon — but as I write the sun is shining out again — and I must get out and drag myself around a little for a change. Farewell, my loving son, till next time. WALT. I send a small bundle of papers.

XIV

Camden, Friday noon, 26th Sept. [1873]. DEAR SON PETE. Your letter of yesterday came this forenoon —

that was a rather serious runaway of cars in the tunnel
week ago — and mighty lucky to get off as you all did —
Pete, I got a few lines from Parker Milburn — he told n
you had a very bad sore on a finger of right hand — the
are plaguey bad things — I am in hopes yours will part
make up in giving you a little resting spell. I sent yo
"the Children of the Abbey," an old novel that used
be all the rage — did you get it? To-day here is a gre
turn out and dedication of the *Masonic Temple* in Phil
delphia — it is truly a handsome and noble building.
rain last night here, and to-day is really perfect. Th
Camden Free Masons marched by here this mornin
about 250, the finest collection of men I thought I ev
saw, but poor music, all brass, a lot of fat young Dutc
men blowing as if they would burst, and making a hell of
hullabaloo — Pete, I am about the same — may be a litt
improved in general strength — had bad spells a goo
deal all the earlier part of the week — some very bad —
but feel better yesterday and to-day — I am making som
calculations of the cool weather — think it may be favo
able to me — did not go out any yesterday — shall try
get out this afternoon a couple of hours — I don't kno
a soul here, — am entirely alone — sometimes sit alor
and think, for two hours on a stretch — have not forme
a single acquaintance here, any ways intimate — M
sister-in-law is very kind in all housekeeping thing
cooks what I want, has first rate coffee for me and som
thing nice in the morning, and keeps me a good bed at

room — all of which is very acceptable — (then, for a fellow of my size, the friendly presence and magnetism needed, somehow, is not here — I do not run foul of any)* — still I generally keep up very good heart — still think I shall get well — When I have my bad spells I wait for them to fade out — I have got a letter from Charley Towner — I am finishing this by the open window — still in the rooms where my mother died, with all the old familiar things — but all drawing to a close, as the new house is done, and I shall move on Monday. WALT.

XV

Camden, Friday afternoon, Oct. 3 [1873]. DEAR PETE, DEAR SON. I received your letter the first of the week, and was interested in your account of your week, of laying off, and of the playing of the band under Schneider and Petrola — also about City R. R. men — I send my love and best respects to all of them — I have had a bad spell again this week — for three days I have had a succession of those *blurs* again — only very much worse than ever before — last night I slept pretty well, and haven't had any of them yet, to-day, but my head feels sore and ready to have them, almost if I move across the room — I am sitting here, feeling pretty bad, my head unsettled and dizzy — I don't go out any more — but am up and

---
* A nautical term = "run up against."

dressed — Still Pete, I do not get discouraged but thin
it will pass over, and I shall feel better, and stron
enough to come back to Washington. Still I don't knov
I think it best to face my situation — it is pretty seriou
I send you a card — and if I should get bad, I will ce
tainly send you word, or telegraph — I will write Monda
or Tuesday next — We have moved into my brother
new house — I am up in the 3rd story room, frontir
south — the sun is shining in bright — it is beautifi
October weather here — My brother had a large roor
very handsome, on second floor, with large bay windo
fronting west, built for me, but I moved up here instea
it is much more retired, and has the sun — I am very cor
fortable here indeed, but my *heart* is blank and lonesom
utterly. 11 *o'clock* A. M. *sitting by the window 1st floo*
I have just been talking with a young married R. R. ma
Thomas Osler, I fell in with — he has a bad bon
gathering on his left hand, a sort of felon, suffere
greatly with it 5 days and nights — had it lanced yeste
day, and is better — he stood by the open window 1
floor, and talked with me, while I sat in an arm-cha
inside — he is a regular R. R. man — you could tell b
the cut of his jib, low collar, cap, clean shirt (for ho
day) dark complexion, and hard dark hands, I took qui
a fancy to him and, *of course*, I suppose he did to me —
believe he works on the locomotive — Pete, you must te
me how you put in the past week — I like such a lett
as your last one — written two or three different times -

It gave me a good idea of what you are doing — and also of how things look in Washington — I have written a line to Col. Hinton and shall write a line to Eldridge.

3 *o'clock* P. M.   My head is feeling very sore and touchy and sensitive — I don't go out — I have re-written my will — What little I have to leave I have left mainly to my lame brother Ed., poor man — Pete, I have left you $200. and my gold watch — (but it will be much better for us to spend the money together, and I have no doubt we shall do so). This house is quite pleasant — it is on the corner — fronts south — side to west — plenty of light and air and view — This afternoon I am quite in hopes I am getting better of my spells to-day, as I have not had any actual spells though I have felt pretty sick all day. But I have been up all day, and eat quite a bite for dinner — Pete, I have written plainly, because I want you to be prepared if anything should happen to me — but I tell you *honest*, I still think I shall pull through — and that I shall be able to write better news early next week — don't you be alarmed yet.   WALT.

XVI

431 *Stevens St. cor. West, Camden, N. J. Thursday noon, Oct.* 9 [1873]. DEAR SON. Your letter of 8th, came this morning — you did perfectly right — I believe you are the greatest comfort I have, and if I get well our love and attachment will be closer than ever. As I write it

CALAMUS

is about noon, and I am sitting up in my room, with window open and the bright sun streaming in. I hav confused spells of the head, and have just had one, last ing about 20 minutes — they are not so bad and pros trating as those of last week — I have to just sit still an wait till they pass over. I eat my breakfast with relis this morning, salmon, graham bread and coffee, etc But did not rest well last night. John Burroughs ha been to see me,— staid a day and night — he has settle up and sold out in Washington and left — He is buildin a home on the Hudson river, 75 miles from N. Y. — ha 10 acres of land on west side of river. I am feelin quite bad to-day about a 13 year old boy, Rob Evans, know here, next door but one — he has had his eye ver badly hurt, I fear it is put out, the doctor has given it u — by an arrow yesterday, the boys playing — I though quite a good deal of him, he would do anything for me — his father was French, and is dead — the boy suffers ver much — and the misfortune is a very, very sad one. I is now ¼ after 12 — and everything looks so sunny an inviting out, I am going to try to get out on the walk fo a few minutes — but I don't navigate as well as I di before I left Washington. *Friday afternoon, ½ past 2* Another beautiful day — I enjoy it, but cannot go aroun in it — I went out yesterday, not far but was badly over come before I got back. At present my head canno stand anything. Still, to-day I am feeling rather bette than usual. I have eaten my dinner — beefsteak an

potatoes, with pumpkin pie and a cup of tea — I eat very moderately but with quite a relish. Dear Pete, serious as these spells are, (and seems as if they *will* continue to come on,) I still have abiding hopes and trust of my recovery yet — though I don't want to be too confident, and wanted you to be prepared for whatever might happen. I shall write a line to-day to Charles Eldridge — I am glad you have got some acquainted with him — I know him thoroughly — he is a thoroughly good and true man — has some ways and notions of his own, but the main things are as *solid* as the hills — Hinton too is a real good, kind man — Now, dear son, don't worry about me — I think in all probability we shall yet be together and that I shall come round to be wholly or partially better — but whichever way it goes with me, it will be all right — your latest two letters have been *first rate* — I read the one before the last, many times, — it is very dear to me.
WALT.

XVII

431 *Stevens St. cor. West, Camden, Oct.* 16 [1873], 2 *p. m.* *Thursday.* DEAR SON. I sent you a postal card yesterday that the bundle had come all right, with the right things I wanted. My condition is still what may be called favorable — that is I still keep up without having any of those decidedly bad spells — blurs, as I call them, of a while ago — and in general I feel as well and as strong (such as it all was) as before I was taken with those

spells. I go out again a little. Pete, I told you about
young railroad man, Tom Osler, 26 years old, that I m
occasionally and talked with, that had a felon on h
hand — I took quite a fancy to him and he to me — We
he is dead, killed instantly — (I have marked the pie
in the paper already sent) — I went around yesterday
where he lived, it is near here, he was married, leaves
young widow, and a nice little two year old boy — I sa
them — his body broken and scalded, lay in the fro
room. Whenever you have the *Star* or *Republican*, on
in a while you can send them (you can send two for
1 c. stamp) I don't mind their being a little old — I s
the *Chronicle* and *Capital* at the reading room — I am fee
ing full as well as usual to-day, and think of going o
and across the ferry — it is so pleasant this afternoo
Friday afternoon — I went out yesterday afternoon -
across to Philadelphia, and up to the Mercantile Libra
Reading Room, I have spoken of. Yesterday, and ye
terday evening I felt better than usual — but am not
well to-day — the worst of my case is these *fall backs* -
But I have been out a little to-day. My walking do
not improve any at all. (Then to make things mo
cheerful, there are many deaths here about from paralysis
I quite miss poor Tom Osler. I am in the habit of s
ting of the forenoon * by the first floor window, readi
the papers and Tom would often stop a few minutes ar
talk to me at the window, on his way to and from tl

* So in MSS.

depot — He would never come in the house, but seemed to like to stop and talk that way with me. My boy that had his eye hurt is doing rather badly too. About myself, my *general strength* not only holds out, but I think rather improves, which helps a good deal. Your postal card came — also a letter from Eldridge enclosing the key. Good bye for this time, my loving boy. WALT.

XVIII

431 *Stevens St. cor. West, Camden, N. J., Oct.* 24 [1873], *Friday afternoon.* DEAR SON PETE. I am still doing as well as when I last wrote — I have many alternations, but upon the whole I have no reason to complain of the last ten days. My head has some bad spells, and a touch or more nearly every day, and my locomotion is still as clumsy as ever — but for all that I am happy in not having any of those spasms of three weeks since, and indeed I have glimpses again of my real self — have had two or three such, of an hour or two each — which I felt very encouraging. Your letter came Tuesday, and I wrote you a few lines on a postal card, which I suppose you received next day. I went to Tommy Osler's, the young R. R. man's, funeral last Sunday — it was near here — poor fellow, he used always to stop a minute at the window and talk off-hand and cheerful — Pete, he often made me think of you, dear son — he was your age and size — he was an only son. I go

CALAMUS

out now about every day, my strength is certain
improving — shall go out this afternoon. About o[ne]
hour ago the big Adams Express wagon drove up to t[he]
door, with a box for me — it was 2 doz 2 lb. cans
fresh Oregon salmon from St. Louis, from my broth[er]
Jeff — I am very fond of it for breakfast, can eat it eve[ry]
day — (my appetite is pretty fair, but I must have ju[st]
the things I want, can't eat any others) — Pete, yo[ur]
description of the old Evangelical alliances fellows, as
they had just walked out of Noah's ark, made me lau[gh]
heartily — you just hit it — I have just got a long lett[er]
from Mrs. O'Connor — she is in Massachusetts — retur[ns]
to Washington in November — How are Mr. and M[rs.]
Nash, and Ed, and all? — give them my love — tell Ed.
shall yet want him to build me *that small house* — I ser[d]
my love to Wash Milburn — I am writing this up in n[y]
room, 3 o'clock, pleasant weather, sun shining, windo[w]
open — I am feeling quite fair to-day. Good bye for th[is]
this time, my loving boy. WALT.

XIX

431 *Stevens St. cor. West, Camden, N. J., Friday aft[er]
noon, Oct.* 31 [1873.] DEAR BOY PETE. My conditio[n]
remains about the same – I don't get ahead any
notice — but I hold my own, as favorable as I ha[ve]
stated in my late letters, and am free yet from the ve[ry]
confused spells of the head and spasms of three week[s]

ago. Besides I think upon the whole, my general strength is the best it has been yet — for an interval every now and then it certainly is. All very encouraging — (But my disease seems to have such ups and downs I have learned to fear to make calculations, almost). The weather here is fine — cool mornings and nights, indeed quite cold at times — but the bulk of the day perfect — I think the cool weather season is beneficial to me. I am sitting here writing this with one of the windows wide open, and the afternoon sun streaming in. I got a letter this morning from Mr. Eldridge that he had paid Godey, my substitute, the money I sent out for his October pay — Washington must be looking pleasant this fall. Write me how you are fixed, and I like to hear all the particulars about your work on the R. R. Good-bye for this time, my loving boy. WALT. It is now a little after 2 — I have had my dinner, beefsteak and potatoes — pumpkin pie and a cup of tea — Don't you think that is doing very well? — It is a glorious afternoon and I am going down to take a trip once or twice across the Delaware in the ferry boat. It makes a pleasant little trip, as the river here is most as wide as the Potomac from 7th St. wharf — has two little islands in the middle, which sometimes we steer between, and sometimes go round — Then *these nights*, Pete — last night I was out, came home about 8 — the moon shining bright as silver — I thought of our old walks, dear son.

CALAMUS

XX

431 *Stevens St. cor. West, Camden, N. Jersey, Sunday aft
noon, Nov.* 9 [1873]. DEAR SON PETE. By accident yo
usual letter was not sent to P. O. so that you could get
Saturday — which may have made you some uneasy
but you need not be, as I still continue to hold my ov
full as good as at previous advices — I still remain cle
of any of those real bad spells of the head.— I canr
walk any better yet — but otherwise am getting alo
very favorably — I received your postal card acknowled
ing the* 10. I get out every fair day — shall go c
about 4 to visit a family here, Col. Johnston, the jolli
man I ever met, an artist, a great talker, but real, natu
first-rate off-hand cheerfulness and comical-sensible ta
a man of good information too, travelled in Europe —
hour or two does me real good - he has a wife, daugh:
and son, all good —I go Sunday evenings to tea —Pe
I send you a paper with a piece in about Richmo
affairs, manufactures, etc., I thought you might like
look over— Here there is great talk of the propos
Centennial Exposition — I will send you pictures of t
buildings soon. I am sitting here in my room 3rd sto
— We have had quite a storm —but at present the s
shines out, by spells — I am feeling quite comfortable
I would almost think of coming back to Washington
but have learned not to make calculations *too soon* or

* The $ omitted in MSS.

sanguine — so I shall remain here for the present — If you see Col. Hinton tell him I am getting along favorably — tell him Mr. Linton, the artist, has lately called upon me — tell Hinton to be sure and come and call on me, should he come to Philadelphia — Tell Wash Milburn, and Parker also, I send them my love, and that I shall be back to Washington this winter — tell Parker I was sorry to hear of his illness — As I write the wind is crooning and whistling around the house at a great rate — it is a music though I like to hear — That is a bad business, the shooting of Ryan and the three good fellows, in Cuba — the Spaniards will probably just keep on at their bloody tricks till the U. S. (and perhaps England) steps in and kicks them out of Cuba — which in my opinion ought to be done without delay — I suppose you knew Ryan by sight, he was around Washington so much — Well, good bye for this time, dear loving boy. WALT.

XXI

431 *Stevens St. cor West, Camden, Friday afternoon, Nov.* 14 [1873]. DEAR PETE, DEAR SON. I am sitting here in my room again writing to you — there is no particular change in the situation — we are having some pretty cold weather here — I go out a little every day, but my walking does not improve any — I had a partially bad spell yesterday afternoon, and did not go out, but it passed over, and to-day I feel as well as I usually have lately —

CALAMUS

I shall get out this afternoon, and over to the Read Room in Philadelphia — (Looking over the papers, I occasionally very interesting *news* about myself — a pa in Salt Lake, Utah, had me dead — and the *Philadel[* *Item*, about the same time had me at a public dinner. Philadelphia, making a speech). I received your last. suppose you got mine last Tuesday — I have just had dinner, bean soup, boiled beef, and pumpkin pie, all g — so you see I might be doing worse — It is now after 2, and I am feeling quite comfortable — and h this will find you all right, my loving boy — WALT.

XXII

431 *Stevens St. cor. West, Camden, N. J., Friday aftern Nov.* 21 [1873]. DEAR SON PETE. Nothing very new me — I continue about the same — my general strer the best it has been yet — I go out a little most e day, but it is very cold weather here — I was quite 1 plus'd at that affair in Bergazzi's with Frank Rives — is he? Is he some one I know? — was he drunk or loc tell me more of it — what he said — the exact words - seems unaccountable to me — from what I gather f your letter you did exactly right. If I hadn't met some queer characters myself — and been the subjec such strange and unaccountable remarks — I sh hardly think anything of the sort possible. — I have o pied myself lately writing — have sent a letter to

Graphic describing the Capitol, which they have accepted, and may publish Saturday or Monday. Have also written a poem which I have sold — will send you one when it appears. — As I write this holding the paper on my lap, I am sitting here in the parlor by the heater — have had my dinner — drank quite a goblet of wine, which I believe has flown into my head. (My brother West and another friend here, have both sent me presents of good wine — and I drink it occasionally, half water — but this time I have taken a little extra) — Pete, I thought I would send you a couple of shirts — so I have ordered them made here, got as near the measure as I could — they will be done in some ten days, perhaps less, and then I will send them. I like mine so well, I have had yours made like them, with collars on. I have had no new togs made this winter. I wear my old gray suit, and the old black overcoat — and when very cold or stormy my gray shawl — If you could see me now leaning against Milburn's counter, you wouldn't *see any difference from last winter* — (but my heart tells a different story) — I have been in all day, and must get out a little — the evenings are the most tedious with me — I can manage to put in *the days*, but these long *cold evenings*. I think if I only had the right quarters in Washington, *my own quarters and a good wood fire, and you with me as* often as possible, I should be comparatively happy. WALT.

CALAMUS

XXIII

431 *Stevens St. cor. West, Camden, N.J., Friday* [*Nov.* 28*th*, [1873] 2 *p. m.* DEAR SON PETE. Here I sit again by the heater in the parlor, writing my weekly letter — I have just had my dinner, some cold turkey and a glas of Missouri wine, etc. Had been out to the P. O. some fiv or six squares distant — but have to take my time — An still getting along very satisfactorily (for I am now satis fied with things not being *very* bad with me) — and m strength is undoubtedly better, which I hope will in tim bring improvement in my walking, and in my head, etc etc. — The letter you spoke of about Penn. av. in th paper was not by me*— In the *Graphic* of Tuesday last Nov. 25, they print a portrait of my beautiful phiz, and criticism on my books, one of the best and friendliest have seen yet — if you can get one in Washington yo will like it — if not you may see it at *Graphic* office i Washington — I have not received any — Also Monday' Nov. 24 *Graphic* prints my letter about the Capitol — Your letter came Tuesday — as I said before you seem t have done what was unavoidable in the Rives muss — but I have a horror of bar room fracases and fights — an I know you have too — As a general thing, I don't thin it necessary to resent the insults of drunkards or fools, — (unless there is something unavoidable in the case) — Did you get the *Scottish Chiefs* I sent? Good bye, m

* *i. e* Was not written by me.

dear, loving boy — I am doing quite well — I hope this will find you feeling well in health and jolly in spirits. WALT.
Pete, I will probably send the shirts early next week by Express.

XXIV

431 *Stevens St. cor. West, Camden, Dec.* 5 [1873], *after* 12 M. DEAR PETE. I am still holding on about the same — it is pretty certain I don't get behindhand, and that's about the best I can say — continue to get out a little every day when the weather will permit — but my walking power is still very bad indeed — Pete, I sent the shirts this morning by Adams express — they are enveloped in a flat paper box about 2 feet long by 1 wide — I hope they will get there Saturday — (but possibly may not reach you till Monday) — (you must pay the freight there) I hope they will fit — the blue one, it wasn't done till last night, is to wear over — I got the stuff, it is first rate Middlesex flannel, cost $5. (same as my summer shirts are made of) — is not intended to be washed often — but can be when necessary — must then be washed by some one experienced in washing nice flannels — I sent *Graphic* with my portrait — (as they sent me some) also my Capitol letter — I received your good letter last Tuesday. Dear son, I send you $10 for your Christmas present — perhaps you will need a pair of winter boots, (or some good cotton flannel for underclothes — or something) — I received a good letter from Mr. Eldridge — Mrs. O'Connor was to come home last Tuesday — I sent

a paper to Parker Milburn with my portrait — also to
Charley Towner — I hope you carried yours up to Mr.
Nash, as I know it would interest and amuse him and Mrs.
Nash — give them both my love — (I see just a line in
the paper that Mr. Nash had given some reminiscences at
a meeting of the oldest inhabitants) — I see the B. and
P. R. R. had a bad freight car accident last Wednesday
night at Patapsco, but no injury to human life or limb —
I have not been quite so well in the head yesterday and
to-day — but am around as usual, as it is nothing very
heavy — We are having a mild spell here, this is the third
day, with partial rain and fog — It is now just after 1 —
I am sitting here writing this in the parlor by the heater
— my dinner is about ready, and I am going — Everything is very complete and correct here — but O, I need
your dear loving face and hand and voice. — Your old
WALT.

XXV

431 *Stevens St. cor. West, Camden, N.J., Dec.* 12 [1873].
DEAR BOY PETE. I felt bad enough to hear of the death
of Bill Burns — and in such a sudden cruel way, — poor
young man — he has had a reckless unsatisfactory life —
many deficiencies and very shiftless — all of which I
understood perfectly well — but I had an affection for
him after all — Have I not heard that he had a wife and
child? which (if so) he has left — but was parted from
quite a while ago — Pete, so your shirts came all safe,
and they fit you, do they? — good — The blue shirt (did

I write?) is to wear *over*, loose — it is made large for that purpose — I like the looks of them, the blue shirt collar turned down low with a nice black silk neck handkerchief, tied loose — over a clean white shirt without necktie — I think they are very becoming to young working men — I sent 3 *Graphics* to Mr. and Mrs. Nash — when you hear, tell me if they came safe — I send you some papers to-day — There is nothing new with me, or my condition — my principal malady is about the same, (no worse) — but I have had for three or four days a wretched cold in the head, sore throat, most lost my voice for two days — everything bad enough — am better rather to-day, begin to speak so I can be understood — shall be all right soon — As I write it is now between 11 and 12 a.m. Friday — it is very mild, sunshiny forenoon — I am sitting here in the parlor — looks south, looks down a pleasant street, West street, full view, makes quite a nice view for me to sit and look out — the letter carrier comes around in about an hour from now, and takes my letters to P. O. — I have become sort of acquainted with most of the carriers, ferry men, car conductors and drivers, etc. etc., they are very good indeed — help me on and off the cars, here and in Philadelphia — they are nearly all young fellows — it all helps along — Well Pete, dear loving boy, I will bid you good bye for this week. WALT.

XXVI

431 *Stevens St. cor. West, Camden, N.J.*, 12 M., *Friday Dec.* 19 [1873]. DEAR BOY PETE. Well, I am sitting here in

the parlor again writing my weekly letter — as I write the rain is pouring and it is a thick and dark day enough — I am feeling pretty bad, but it seems to be mostly from a severe cold in the head — any how I am having one of my bad spells, of which I have gone through so many — had a bad night last night — but have eat my breakfas' this morning, and have no doubt I shall feel better before many days. Pete, I received your letter and the *Herald* last Monday all right. Did Mr. and Mrs. Nash get the 3 *Graphics* I sent them? — I have been out most every day the past week, and have been across the river to Phil adelphia — It has been a very pleasant week, and I have enjoyed sailing across the Deleware, and the splendid sunsets most every evening — it is my greatest enjoyment — Pete, all you write about folks and things in Washing ton is interesting to me — it will be read, everything you scratch down, as I sit here a great deal of the time, (and time is dull and lonesome at the best) — My pieces I have written (I believe I mentioned about it) have not yet appeared in the Magazine — but the money has been paid me for them, and they are in type, and I have read the proofs — I will either send them to you, when printed, or send you word, so you can get them yourself — Did I send you both my letters about the Capitol in the *Graphic?* — I believe I did, but if not I can yet — I send you to day's Philadelphia *Press* — nothing special in it — Well, good bye for this time, dear loving boy. WALT. Pete. how about running on here to see me for a day or two? —

Couldn't you come, convenient, say latter part of next week? If you can, I will fix the time.

XXIV

431 Stevens St. cor. West, Camden, N.J., Dec. 26 — Noon [1873]. DEAR BOY PETE. I have been looking for you the last two days and nights — but I have about given you up now. I have been kept in pretty close, as we have had real winter here, snow and bad weather, and bad walking — I have been quite alone, as my brother and sister went off to Delaware on Wednesday on a Christmas visit, to return to-morrow Saturday — I am about the same — my strength still keeps quite encouraging — I think is better than any time yet — my walking no better, and still a good deal of distress in the head — but as I said in my letter of Monday last, (did you get it Tuesday?) — I somehow feel a little more like myself than any time since I was taken down — Your last letter was quite a treat — so much about Washington, and folks, one thing and another — As I write I sit here in the parlor — we have had an awful time from the fire going out in the heater, and making it up again — there is so much complicated machinery about one of these heaters with all the late improvements — give me my old stove and wood fire yet — It is snowing by fits here this morning. WALT.

A GLIMPSE through an interstice caught,
Of a crowd of workmen and drivers in a bar-room around the
    stove late of a winter night, and I unremark'd seated in a
    corner,
Of a youth who loves me and whom I love, silently approaching
    and seating himself near, that he may hold me by the hand,
A long while amid the noises of coming and going, of drinking
    and oath and smutty jest,
There we two, content, happy in being together, speaking little,
    perhaps not a word.

                                          Leaves of Grass (Ed'n 1892), p. 109.

LETTERS OF 1874

I

431 *Stevens St. cor. West, Camden, N.J., Jan.* 2, 12 M. [1874]. DEAR BOY. I am about the same — consider myself improving, if anything, though slowly enough — Pete, I will get you the Dictionary, I will see about it soon. You spoke about the post of baggage master on the through New York train — and the appointment being in Philadelphia. Who appoints them? Tell me more fully about it in your next. I got your last letter, and several papers. To-day I have received a letter from Charles Eldridge — we have had a long rainy and dark time here, but mild — no snow on the ground now — I go out — As I write, the trains are going by, about 400 feet off, ringing and smoking — there are 20 a day in full view from here. WALT. I send you a picture for your New Year's.

II

431 *Stevens St. cor. West, Camden, Jan.* 9 [1874]. WELL PETE, MY DEAR LOVING BOY. I have just come in from a 15 minutes walk outside, with my little dog — it is now ½ past 1 Friday afternoon — the bright sun shining, and the air and everything as pleasant as one could wish — (after most a week of rainy, dark and disagree-

CALAMUS

able but warmish weather) — I have the same old sto
to tell, — and thankful enough to have nothing worse
communicate — it is probable I am really slowly gaini
— though I have occasional bad spells yet. Your lett
was received — I was thinking whether something cou
not be done about getting the position of through bagga
master — and feel inclined to try for you — (you kn
there is nothing of that sort done without trying) — L
you get the story " Rolling Stone " I sent by P. O.? —
have had a visitor from New York this forenoon —
old acquaintance, a printer and foreman, I knew 20 yea
ago, very sickly and expecting to die, at that time — n
quite lively and well, really jolly and magnetic, and go
company, and a good fellow, (like Parker Milburn) —
have an occasional visitor, but not many — Pete, if y
see anybody coming to Philadelphia you think I wou
like to see, give 'em my address — I am glad to see m
any one for a change — Your old WALT.

III

431 *Stevens St. cor. West, Camden, N.J., Friday forenc
11 ½* [*16th Jan.* 1874]. Well, son, how do you make c
this cold weather? for I suppose you are having it the
as we are here — we had quite a snow storm here thr
or four nights ago, and since then it has cleared off bit
cold, — (thermometer at 10 above an hour ago, at c
west door) — Still I go out some, though very stiff — a
lately some spells in my head rather bad and queer, wl

LETTERS OF 1874

I have said in former letters about my general strength still holds good — otherwise I am in a bad way yet, and don't consider myself out of the woods, have not been so well as usual the last week. If you come across the *Weekly Graphic* just out get it, as I have commenced a series of pieces about things just before and during the war. The series is to continue through four or five numbers. Get one for Mr. and Mrs. Nash — Pete, I received the *Golden Grain* — also the letter, *Herald*, and *Repub.* — send me one of the latter, occasionally — I had rather have it than any — (but you needn't put yourself out to get it) — As I write the sun is shining bright and clear as can be — the ground is white with snow in all directions, it is not melting anywhere — as I crossed the river yesterday toward dusk, the old fellow, the chargè* of the ferry house, told me that between 12 and 2 o'clock the previous night over 30 persons crowded in there, poor houseless creatures, to keep from freezing to death — he keeps a great stove red hot all night — some were young, some old, some evidently real respectable people — the orders are to not allow it, but he hadn't the heart to turn 'em out — God help the homeless and moneyless this weather.
WALT.

IV

431 *Stevens St. cor. West, Camden, N. Jersey, Jan.* 19, *Monday noon* [1874]. DEAR LOVING SON. I received your

* Intended for chargé

letter this forenoon. Pete, I thought I would send yo
little change enclosed — all I have by me to-day — (I
I have plenty at my command) — It is wet and fog
to-day, and a glaze of ice everywhere — so I am compell
to remain in. I am feeling decidedly better the last
hours — am surely getting through the winter very w
— guess I shall come out with the frogs and lilacs in
spring — I keep a bully good heart, take it altogether
and you must too my darling boy. WALT.

V

431 *Stevens St. cor. West, Camden, N. Jersey, Frid*
1 ½ P.M. [*Jan. 23rd,* 1874]. DEAR BOY PETE. Y
letter came Wednesday — you must try to cultivate a
keep up a gay and cheerful heart, and shed off bothe
tions, and the impositions of employers, etc., as a du
sheds water in a rain storm — that's the best capital
fellow can have through his whole life, I find. I am o
so-so — had a very bad night last night — it's a tough p
Pete — still I think I shall come out of it. We are h
ing it very mild here now — after snow and cold the fi
of the week — too mild, like April to-day, cloudy a
some rain. I keep myself some busy writing * — hav
piece in *Harper's Monthly* just out (February) — sh
have another in the March number — Can't seem to
without occupying my mind through the day — nights

* *i. e.* I keep writing more or less.

worst for me — I can't rest well — has been so now for a month — But I must not fill my letter with my complaints — To-day is just a year since I was paralyzed (23rd Jan. '75) — What a year it has been to me — Good bye, my loving boy — write me all the news and gossip. WALT.

VI

431 *Stevens St. cor. West, Camden, N. Jersey, Friday afternoon, Jan. 30, 2 o'clock* [1874]. DEAR PETE. I am having another of my bad spells to-day — but it will pass over — I have had a pretty good time most of the week till last night — thought I was getting decidedly better — (and guess I am yet, and that this will pass over). Everything goes on the same with me here. As I write this I am sitting here alone as usual in the parlor by the heater — I have just been out, but it was so chilly and raw I didn't venture off the block, but came back in 5 or 6 minutes — the air feels like snow. The trains of the Camden and Amboy are going by on the track about 50 or 60 rods from here, puffing and blowing — often train after train, following each other — and locomotives singly, whisking and squealing, up the track and then down again — I often sit here and watch them long — and think of you. I think I shall try again to get out, evening* — sometimes it makes me feel better, after I get out in the open air, and move around a little. *7.15 evening,*

* In the evening.

CALAMUS

Friday — I am writing this over in the Mercan
Library, 10th St. Philadelphia — I have felt better si
4 o'clock and have come out and crossed the river, a
taken quite a ride up Market St. 2 miles in the Mar
St. cars. The cars are very nice, old style, cushion
fare 7 cents — if you get a transfer you have to pay ex
— the working hours are from 16½ to 18 — they h:
the new alarm punch, every fare or ticket, rings a li
bell every time you punch — I suppose you have see
— they say it is quite a success, and they are introd
ing them in other cities — but it will get played out
Pete write how you are getting along — and all about
folks, every one I know — I am feeling as well as ust
as I finish this letter — Good bye for this time my lov:
son. — WALT. Don't you get discouraged at work, or
the road — I feel that we shall yet be together, and h;
good times, just being with each other, no matter h
poor.

VII

431 *Stevens St. cor. West, Camden, N. Jersey*, Fri
noon, Feb. 6 [1874]. DEAR BOY PETE. Both your lett
came this week — also one from my friend Eldridge,
too speaks of meeting and talking with you. It is r
winter here, the ground all covered with snow, as I lo
out — not the least thaw to-day, as it is cloudy — I r
pretty late mornings — had my breakfast a little wh
ago, mutton-chop, coffee, nice brown bread and sw

butter, very nice — eat with very fair appetite — I enjoy my breakfast better than any other meal — (eat a light dinner pretty late, and no supper) — Feel generally about the same as before described — no worse no better, (nothing to brag of anyhow). I have mentioned about my crossing the ferry — from our house the cars run by the next corner, (200 feet or less) a half mile or so to the ferry — the Delaware here is full three quarters of a mile wide — it is a noble river, not so wide as the Potomac nor with fine banks like Arlington, but grander, and with more style, and with powerful rushing tides, now great processions of broken ice, many little and some great big cakes — the boats are very fine and strong, go crashing right ahead, with a loud noise, breaking the cakes often a foot thick and more — I enjoy crossing these days — it does me good — the ferry men are all very kind and respectful — I have been reading a book *Merrie England in the Olden Time*, a London book, with pictures, full of fun and humor — I have enjoyed it much — There is an awful amount of want and suffering from no work, here about — a young man was here yesterday — had seen me in Washington — wanted help — I gave him a little — I see the cars and locomotives skurrying by as I close. WALT.

VIII

431 *Stevens St. cor West, Camden, N. Jersey, Feb.* 13, 2½ P. M. [1874]. DEAR PETE. Here I am yet in my

CALAMUS

big chair in the parlor — I am up and around, but
very well — I am having a return, (though not so sever
of those old *blurs* that used to trouble me — have ha
succession of them all day to-day so far — begun yest
day — but I have no doubt they will pass over. It
cloudy and sulky here to-day, partially thawing — and
raining now — I have been out, managed to walk arou
the block, but had to return — did not feel well. Pe
there is nothing new — I got your last letter — have
ceived letters from Mrs. O'Connor — I have no doub
shall feel better — my sickness comes and goes and
relief spells the same — I shall probably have to stay
the rest of the day and evening, which is very dull a
stupid for me — in fact quite dismal — But I must r
write what will make you blue, would rather cheer y
up — I am still continuing the pieces in the *Wee
Graphic* (will be ended with one or two more) — expe
to have a piece in next *Harper* (March), but am not c
tain. — Just as I close the carrier has tapped at the w
dow — he brings me a letter from Boston, and in it
check, paying a debt due me a long time, and which
had quite given up — which puts me in better spirits
good bye for present my dear, loving son — your WAL

IX

431 *Stevens St. cor. West, Camden, N. Jersey, Fria
afternoon*, 2 ½ [*Feb.* 20, 1874]. DEAR BOY PETE. W
Pete, dear son, I have just had my dinner (stewed chick

and onions — good) and here I sit again in the same old chair, in the parlor, writing my weekly screed to you — Nothing to brag of this week — have passed a disagreeable week — mainly I suppose from a bad, bad cold in the head — have suffered badly from it, every way — but keep up and around — and shall get through with it, when the time comes — Have not written any for publication the past fortnight — have not felt at all like writing — My *Weekly Graphic* pieces are about concluded — (the next week's, the 6th number, ends them — I am just reading the last proof to-day) — I have a poem in the March *Harper**— as I believe I mentioned in my last, (I am told that I have colored it with thoughts of myself — very likely) — Pete, I received your letter last Monday — and *Herald* — I have not sent you any papers or books lately — but will, again — As I sit here, concluding this, I am feeling quite comfortable. Take care of yourself, my darling boy — your old WALT, as always. Pete, as I am a little in extra funds to-day I enclose you $5. — thinking (like Mrs. Toodle's coffin) it "might perhaps come in use sometime"

X

431 *Stevens St. cor. West, Camden, N. Jersey, Feb.* 27 [1874]. DEAR SON. Nothing very different or new with me — I have had rather a hard week, (continued

* "*The Prayer of Columbus.*"

CALAMUS

from the former one)—but still I don't get *flat*—a:
often thankful to be as well as I am—I received you
letter and paper.—We too have had the same sno
storm I see you have had in Washington—it is brigl
and sunny to-day here, though middling cool—I am si
ting here in the parlor alone—it is about 10—I hav
had my breakfast—I amuse myself by seeing the locom
tives and trains go by—I see them very plainly out
the back window—they are only 7 or 800 feet off—the
go by constantly—often one right after another—
have got used to them and like them—Did you see n
last pieces in the *Weekly Graphic?* (the sixth paper, ju
out, is the last)—I sent you a couple of Philadelph
papers yesterday—I was glad you wrote me about Was
Peddrick—I have not heard from him in a long time—(l
did me a good turn once in the office, just out of god
will, and I shall never forget it)—Pete, write whoev
you see, and about anything in Washington—I met
young man here from Washington last night, W'm. Colei
an engineer in the fire room Treasury *—Love to M
and Mrs. Nash—and to Parker and Wash Milburn-
and in short to all my friends—your old WALT.

XI

431 *Stevens St. cor. West, Camden, N. Jersey, March*
[1874]. DEAR BOY PETE. I was quite shocked to he

* *i. e.* in the fire room of the Treasury Building.

of Parker Milburn's death — he was never very rugged, but he kept up so well, and always had some cheerful, lively thought or saying — I was far from anticipating this — I think he had very noble traits, and both you and I liked him thoroughly — Pete, I hope he is better off — I will try to write a few words to Wash — Pete I have received both your letters — I go out often in the Market St. cars past the West Philadelphia depot you speak of, but never get out or go in there, as it is a great depot, full of hurrying people, and hacks and drivers, and trains coming and going continually and people rushing and crowding — too much excitement for me — So you saw Colein, in the Treasury — I saw him only a few minutes in a street car, but he could give you some report of me from his own eyes, and that I know satisfied you better — I am feeling quite an improvement, or let up, the last two days and nights on the bad spell I spoke of in my last letters — have slept better the last two nights. To-day as I write here, it is cloudy and feels a little like snow coming — it has been very mild here too — Pete, go up sometime when you start out early in the afternoon and see Mrs. O'Connor, 1015 O street near 11th — she will be very glad to see you. I hope you won't fail to go. I am feeling quite comfortable to-day as I write. Pete, I sometimes think if I was fixed so that I had you with me every day I should get well — good bye for this week, my loving son — from your old WALT.

CALAMUS

XII

431 *Stevens St. cor. West, Camden, N. Jersey,* Thursday 5 ½ P. M. [*March* 12, 1874]. DEAR BOY PETE. I have bee in all day, I don't think I ever knew such long continue gales of wind — this is now the fourth or fifth day - night and day — and as I write it is howling and whir ing just as bad as ever — I havn't been out any to spea of for three days — the gales are too much for me. M spell of let up and feeling more comfortable continue with some interruptions — night before last, and for son time yesterday I was in a bad way again — but had good night's rest last night, and am comfortable to-day - I think I am decidedly more improving than going behin hand — I have thought frequently of Parker Milburn - all his ways and his good points come up in my mind - and now the news comes of the sudden death of M Sumner — Your letter came Monday and the *Herald*. - *Friday, March* 13, 12 M. Not very well to-day — To ad to my troubles a very bad cold in the head and all ove me, again — this is the third attack this winter — bu enough of grunting — The papers are filled with Sun ner's* death, funeral, life, etc. The cold, dry gale co tinues here. I get letters from Mrs. O'Connor. Don fail to go up and make her a call, when convenient. Yc remember Arnold Johnson that used to live over on th

* Charles Sumner, anti-slavery statesman and United Stat Senator from Massachusetts, b. at Boston 1811, d. 1874.

hill by the Insane Asylum — well he has come back to Washington, and is Chief Clerk again Light House Board, and Wm. O'Connor has changed to a clerkship in the Library Treasury.* I am sitting here alone in the same old seat in the parlor writing. Good bye for this time dear boy. WALT.

XIII

431 *Stevens St. Camden, March* 20, 4 ½ P.M. [1874]. DEAR BOY PETE. Nothing particular or new in my condition — I have been to the Doctor's to-day — had quite a long interview — no great satisfaction — I still have pretty uncomfortable times — and yet I keep up good heart in the main. I will make out only a short letter this time, I see. Good bye my loving son, I will try to do better next week. WALT.

XIV

431 *Stevens St. cor. West, Camden, N. Jersey,* [*March* 26, 1874] *Thursday afternoon* 2 ½. I have just had my dinner — roast beef, lima beans, graham bread and sweet butter, with a cup of tea, and some stewed cranberries — I eat quite a good dinner, and enjoyed it all. I still consider myself getting along very well. O, if this only holds out, and keeps on favorably, even if ever so moderate and slow — But I seem to have so many of these gleams

* The library of the Treasury Department?

CALAMUS

that delude me into thinking I am on the way to re
covery, but soon cloud over again, and let me back a
bad as ever — But every time I feel pretty easy, I sti
keep thinking, *now* I am *certainly* going to get muc
better this time. Pete, your short letter came to-day
written on the cars — dear son, come whenever you car
As I said on my postal card, if you were here this weel
you would find me more like myself, (with the exceptio
of walking) than I have been for fourteen months —
whether it will continue or not, God only knows — bu
we will hope for the best. As I sit here writing to yo
to-day, it appears to me every way hopeful, and likel
that we shall yet have good times. Everything is quie
rather lonesome. My little dog is stretched out on th
rug at full length, snoozing. He hardly lets me go
step without being close at my heels — follows me in m
slow walks, and stops or turns just as I do. We hav
had a most windy blustering March, but it is pleasante
and milder yesterday and to-day —(I saw the new moo
over my right shoulder a week ago, — *of course* a sur
sign of good luck) — Will finish this letter and send
to-morrow. *Friday, March* 27, *noon.* Pleasant and brigl
weather — have been out on the sidewalk in front, onc
or twice, with my shawl around me — walk slow an
quite feeble — have some spells of bad headache — Wer
by the West Philadelphia depot yesterday afternoon, i
the Market Street horse cars — saw plenty of R. R. me
and conductors about the place, lounging and waitin

their time — thought if I could only see you among them — as I sit here writing I can see the trains of the Camden and Amboy, in full view, some 40 or 50 rods off — makes it quite lively — As I write, I am feeling pretty comfortable, and am going out awhile after I finish this — but had a bad night last night. Hope this will find you all right — good bye for this time, dear son.
WALT.

XV

431 *Stevens St. cor. West, Camden, N. Jersey, April* 10, 12 M. [1874]. DEAR PETE. Nothing very new or different in my condition, or anything else — have hardly been doing as well since I last wrote, as before — but still hope to pull up. — Received your letter last Monday, and the *Herald*. Not much of a letter this time, my loving boy — as I don't seem to be able to write much — though, as I sit here, I am not feeling any worse than usual. Ashton has lost his little child : died last Thursday. I have just received two letters from Mrs. O'Connor. How does all go with you? Pete, darling, shan't I send you a little money? WALT.

XVI

431 *Stevens St. cor. West, Camden, N. Jersey, April* 16, 1 P.M. [1874]. DEAR SON. I send you a letter a day ahead this week — Nothing new with me — received the letter of last Sunday — also the *Capital* and the *Herald* —

I had a day or two's visit, very acceptable, from John Bur
roughs last Saturday and Sunday — he has built a hous
on the Hudson River about 80 miles from N. Y. has
little farm there, 9 or 10 acres, very nice — As I write
am feeling comfortable, (but every day and every nigh
seems to bring its bad spell, or several of them) — Some
how I still feel that I shall come round, and that we shal
be together and have some good times again — but
don't know. Your WALT.

XVII

431 *Stevens St. Camden, N. Jersey, May* 1, 2 P.M
[1874]. DEAR PETE. I have been out halting aroun
for a walk, as it is quite pleasant to-day — But I believ
I have overdone the matter, as I have a pretty bad fee
ing the last hour or two both in the head and left side
and as I sit here writing. So your limited express seem
to be a real success — if it keeps up as well as it ha
begun I have no doubt it will increase, and be patror
ized, and become a permanent institution — (I had go
the idea, somehow, at first that the same crew wer
through from Washington to New York, and so was som
in hopes of seeing you in Philadelphia) — No change i
my condition or prospects — the young man, Walte
Godey, still works as my substitute in the Solicitor'
office — I haven't had any word from Eldridge in tw
months, nor from Mrs. O'Connor in some time — (hav
you been up there?) — Do you see Hinton or Tasistro

— My sister has just called me to my dinner — so I will close for this time. Your old WALT.

XVIII

431 *Stevens St. cor. West, Camden, N. Jersey. May 22, 3¼ P.M.* [1874]. DEAR PETE. I hope you will be able to come, as you said in your last — If I knew when and where you would arrive in Philadelphia, I would try to meet you — As I wrote you before, you must come to Market St. ferry, Philadelphia, a mile and a half or 2 miles from R. R. depot, and cross over by boat to Federal St., Camden — (The Philadelphia horse cars run Sundays — run down to the foot of Market St. — but the Camden ones do not — but it is not very far from the ferry in Camden). I am very much the same — my being disabled and want of exercise for 16 months, (and many other wants too) have saddled me with serious dyspepsia and what the doctor calls gastric catarrh, very obstinate, causing me really more suffering and pain than my paralysis — but though I have had spells enough, thank God I also have middling good ones — and as I write this have just had my dinner, nice salt oysters, raw, fresh, and am feeling quite comfortable — Dear son, I shall look for you. WALT.

XIX

431 *Stevens St. cor. West, Camden, N. Jersey, June 25* [1874]. DEAR BOY PETE. I have weathered it out pretty well

this week — at present moment I am sitting here cover'
with sweat, with nothing on but shirt and pants — to-da
and yesterday the very hottest kind — I suppose you hav
it too.— Pete, there is nothing new in my case, and n
prospect more than usual of anything *sudden* — but
seems pretty clear that there is no substantial recover
probable, (hardly possible) for me — how long it will la
this way it is of course impossible to tell — I take it a
without growling — things are steadily growing worse wi
me — But I must not worry you — and may-be there is som
thing more favorable ahead — I busy myself a little eve
day writing — I want to fix my books in a little bett
shape, this summer — partly busy with a new volume -
so that they will all be comprised in two volumes — (n
very much really new matter, but some) — So you dor
come on to Baltimore now, (as I take it from your last
— Love to you, dear son. WALT. Love to Mr. and M:
Nash — Do you ever see Mrs. O'Connor or Eldridge? -
Is Tasistro still around?

XX

431 *Stevens St. cor. West, Camden, N. Jersey, July* 1
[1874]. DEAR, DEAR SON. I am still here sufferir
pretty badly — have great distress in my head, and a
almost steady pain in left side — but my worst troubl
let up on me part of the time — the evenings are my be
times — and somehow I still keep up in spirit, and, (th
same old story) *expect* to get better. I have been di

charged from my clerkship in the solicitor's office, Treasury, by the new Solicitor, Mr. Wilson. I think of laying up here in Camden, I have bought a cheap lot — and think of putting up a little two or three room house for myself, my darling son, you must not be unhappy about me — I hope and trust things may work so that we can yet be with each other, at least from time to time — and meanwhile we must adapt ourselves to circumstances. You keep on and try to do right, and live the same square life you always have, and maintain as cheerful a heart as possible, and as for the way things finally turn out, leave that to the Almighty — Pete, I shall want you or Mr. Eldridge to see to the sending on here of my boxes at Dr. White's — I will write further about it — I have not heard anything from Eldridge, or Mrs. O'Connor, or any of the Washington folk for quite a long time. Have you been up to see Mrs. O'C. ? Pete, didn't you get my last Saturday's postal card ? I wrote you one, I got yours last Monday — Did you get the Camden paper with my College piece in ? I sent one. Very hot here yesterday and to-day. I don't fret at all about being discharged — it is just as well — I wonder it didn't come before — How are your folks at home? — your dear mother and all — write about all and Mr. and Mrs. Nash, Wash Milburn, and the R R. boys. Your old WALT.

CALAMUS

XXI

431 *Stevens St. Camden, Aug.* 28 [1874]. DEAR PET
Nothing very new with me — rather a mixed week — son
suffering — Pete, if you have a decided wish to go on tl
Pullman car, and are pretty clear that it would be a go⟨
move, I will let you have $100. Good bye for this tim
dear son. Your WALT.

XXII

Camden, Friday afternoon [*Aug.* 29, 1874]. DE,
PETE. I still remain about the same, and with nothi:
to write about in the way of my improvement, or anythi:
else — but I thought you would want to have wor
Your letter of last Sunday came all right. The pap
has also come. I am no worse — and continue to li
on hope — fortunately I have been stocked with a go⟨
plentiful share of it. It is pleasant weather here, thou|
hot — we have frequent rains — we have had one to-dɛ
about an hour ago, but now it is very bright and plei
ant — I am going to try to get out a little — So go⟨
bye for this time, dear son — I hope to write more of
letter next time. WALT.

XXIII

431 *Stevens St. cor. West, Camden, N. J., Oct.*
[1874]. DEAR PETE. I want some things taken out
my trunk, and put in a bundle and sent here by expres

LETTERS OF 1874

I have written to-day to Mr. Eldridge and sent him the key. I have asked him to go into Milburn's between 3.30 and 4 this afternoon, and meet you — or if not convenient for you this afternoon, to-morrow or next will do just as well, as I am in no hurry — you both go up in my room and get them — I want my old gray suit, coat, vest and, (I think there are two pair of pants) my old black overcoat that is laid away in the trunk. Black felt hat — (the smallest lightest one). The old buckskin gloves. I think some big sheets of very stout wrapping paper, and plenty of stout cord will do — the directions must be very plain and in two places — If not convenient to go to-day, go to-morrow afternoon, or next. I don't want the freight paid, as I will pay it on delivery here. I enclose a dollar as there may be some expense (some little fixings). Pete, I received your letter this morning, and it was very welcome, as always. I received the *Sunday Herald* too. I am having a good spell so far to-day — (if it would only continue) — The bundle will come well enough, as it is a short straight route, if you only do it up so they won't get loose, and put on plain directions. WALT.

CAMERADO, I give you my hand!
I give you my love more precious than money,
I give you myself before preaching or law.

       Leaves of Grass (Ed'n 1892), p. 129.

LETTERS OF 1875

I

431 *Stevens St. cor. West, Camden, N. Jersey*, Friday, 2 P. M. [1875]. DEAR PETE. Nothing special to write you, about myself, or anything else, this week, your letter and the *Herald* came last Monday. The time goes very tedious with me — and yet I think I am getting better, (but don't know for sure) — Still have frequent bad spells. I stopt at the W. Philadelphia depot, Market street, two or three evenings ago, in the general passengers' room, to rest, about 10 minutes. Then took the car for Market St. ferry, (a mile and a half or three quarters) and over to Camden, home — I get desperate at staying in — not a human soul for cheer, or sociability or fun, and this continued week after week and month after month — So you met Johnny Saunders in Baltimore, and he is flourishing. If you see him again, tell him to write to me — he is a young man I always loved. ½ *past* 2. I have just had a nice oyster stew for my dinner — it is blustering weather, partly clear, partly cloudy, and one or two little flirts of snow to-day. I send you a paper or two, but nothing in them. I will try to stop in Philadelphia and find that little dictionary I promised you — So long, my loving son, your old WALT.

CALAMUS

II

431 *Stevens St. cor. West, Camden, N. Jersey, Apri, noon* [1875]. DEAREST SON. I saw the R. R. sn the first thing in the paper in the morning, and run eyes over the account with fear and trembling — only on reading it over a second time was I satisfied you were not in it — poor souls! for I suppose every that was in it, had some who heard or read the news pain and terror — some parent, wife, friend, or chil poor Buchanan — but I hope from accounts that he get up again, before long without serious damage — papers here publish full, and I guess very good acco of the whole affair — I liked what the *Star* said so pla — that *the cause below all others* of such accidents, is cause they run such a route *over a single track* — may remember my warning on the same point three y ago in a talk with you. Pete, the spring finds pretty much in the same tedious and half way condi I have been lingering in now over two years — up around every day, look not much different, and eat pi well — but not a day passes without some bad sp sometimes *very bad*, and never a real good night's s — yet still I have a sort of feeling not to give it up — keep real good spirits — don't get blue, even at worst spells — I am sitting here to-day as usual alon the front room, by the window — feel pretty comfort — the weather is bright and pleasant here to-day, cool for the season, and the most backward I have

LETTERS OF 1875

known — My sister is going away for some ten days tomorrow or next day, and I shall be quite alone in the house — wish you could come on and pay me a visit — Would you like to have me direct any letters or papers to the American Hotel, Balt., or shall I just direct to you at Washington as usual? — love to my darling son.
WALT.

III

431 *Stevens St. cor. West, Camden, N. Jersey, Aug.* 6 [1875]. DEAR PETE, DEAR, DEAR BOY. Still here, pulling through the summer — (I think the winter is better for me) the hot sunny days are worst for me — an extra bad strange feeling every day in the head, (the doctor thinks probably the result of an old sunstroke 20 years ago — now the brain liable to it again in its sensitive condition) — otherwise not much different — *bad enough though*. I still go out a little (most always feel at the best, for me, evenings, from sundown to 10.) Papers, etc., came. I still keep a little at work — there is a printing office here, where I am doing my work — they are young men of the right stripe, and very kind and considerate and respectful to me — fix every thing in type, proof, etc., just to suit me — I am leisurely preparing my new volume. Mr. Marvin, an Internal Revenue Clerk, a friend of mine, has stopt and paid me a visit on his return to Washington. Plenty of rain here — hot but pleasant to-day — What has become of Tasistro? — Pete, you haven't made that call on

CALAMUS

Mrs. O'C. yet. Come when you can, my darling bo
Your loving old comrade and father. WALT W.

IV

431 *Stevens St. cor. West, Camden, N. Jersey, Aug.* 1
[1875]. DEAR SON. I am not feeling very bright to-da
— hardly capable of writing a cheerful letter — and
don't want to send you a blue one — will feel better b
next time, your WALT.

V

Camden, Aug. 29 [1875]. MY DEAR SON. Your lette
came all right last Monday, and the papers. Send m
the *Herald* tomorrow, (with one blue stamp on) yo
needn't mind the other Sunday papers — I send yo
Harper's Magazine for September — I am still holding m
own — gain a little strength, and am certainly improvin
though very slowly — both head and leg are bad enough
but general feeling is much better, most of the time —
have sent Philadelphia papers once or twice and ma
again — There is nothing in them, but I thought yo
would know I was still around — The weather here i
pleasant, and cool enough, favorable to me — I get ou
a little every day — am going out when I finish this —
Cannot write much to-day — am having a bad head-ach
all day — still I feel in good heart. So long, Pete, dea
boy. WALT.

LETTERS OF 1875

VI

Camden, Nov. 3 [1875]. DEAR BOY. I have received your letter, and enclose the $10. for you. I am still the same — am all alone in the house to-day, as my brother has gone to New York and my sister has gone somewhere visiting to spend the day. How I wish you were here to-day. WALT.

VII

431 *Stevens St. cor. West, Camden, N. Jersey, Dec.* 3, *noon* [1875]. DEAR PETE, DEAR SON. I am getting over my late bad spell — I have been very sick indeed, the feeling of death and dizziness, my head swimming a great deal of the time — turning like a wheel — with much distress in left side, keeps me awake some nights all night — the doctor says, however, these troubles, in his opinion, are from a very serious and obstinate *liver affection* — not from head, lungs, heart — he still thinks there is nothing but what I will get the better of — (and we will trust he is a true prophet) — I wrote about like the foregoing to Mrs. O'Connor, but was too sick to repeat it to you — and that was one reason I asked you to go up there,* — I havn't been out for three weeks, but ventured out yesterday for an hour, and got along better than I expected — and shall go out, or try to, to-day as it is very pleasant —

---

* Had doubtless written a letter to Mrs. O'Connor and a postcard to Pete.

CALAMUS

you must not be needlessly alarmed, my darling boy, fc
I still think I shall get, at any rate partially well an
strong enough — The doctor is quite encouraging —
comes every day— and I feel a good heart yet — M
young fireman friend Alcott (I think I mentioned hi
sickness) is dead and buried, poor fellow — I send yo
a bit of piece of mine about him from the paper —I hav
some spurts of visits, and company — but very little th:
goes to the right spot with me — My brother George ha
got a horse and light wagon and takes me out now an
then, I enjoy it much — but I have been too feeble latel
— Altogether pretty lonesome here, but might be muc
worse — Love to Mr. and Mrs. Nash, and to all inquirin
friends.   Your old WALT.

LETTERS OF 1876-1880

I

CAMDEN, N. J. [*Wednesday,*] *Dec.* 13 [1876]. DEAREST PETE. I ought to have written to you before — but I believe lazy and listless fits grow stronger and frequenter on me as I get older — and then I don't do anything at all, especially just the things I ought to do. But I often, often think of you boy, and let that make it up. I certainly am feeling better this winter, more strength to hold out, walking or like, than for nearly now four years — bad enough yet, but still *decidedly better* (my loving boy, I underscore the words, for I know they will make you feel good, to hear).

I heard about the accident on the road at the time two weeks ago — and was uneasy enough until I heard definite particulars — such things seem the fortune of R. R. travel, which I sometimes think more risky than the "fortune of war," which the knowing ones know well is more chance and accident (I mean the victory in battles) than it is generalship.

Pete, I am sitting up here alone in my room 8 o'clock P. M. writing this — I am feeling quite comfortable — I stood the cold snap of the last three days very well — to-day has been moderate and nice here — Nothing new or special in my affairs — I am selling a few of my books,

CALAMUS

(the new, 2 vol., 10 dollar, edition) from time to time - mostly to English and Irish purchasers — it is quite fun) how many of my books are sent for from Ireland. Lo to you, dearest son. WALT.

II

431 *Stevens Street, Camden, Dec.* 27, '76. DEAR So The money came all right, and I will keep it for t] present, and use it for myself — *but only to return it some future time when I am flush.* Nothing very new wi me. I still feel pretty well, for me, (and considering t] past four years). Who knows? May be after this winte I shall feel well enough to come on to Washingto and make out several weeks — and we'll have a go time together, my loving son, —(no more long walks be sure — but we can be happy other ways) — Beautift mild, sunny, thawing afternoon to-day — I have been o a little — down to see a poor young man, an oysterma Jim Davis, very low with consumption, took him son stewed chicken for his dinner — then went to a nice rea ing room and library we have here, very handy — the home to my own dinner, stewed chicken and nice roa potatoes — and now (2½) up stairs in my room writir this, and feeling very fair — O Pete, you get that ar chair (with the broken arm) I left at Mrs. Nash's ·· pe haps the broken arm is still there, if so get it put on - then take the chair home for you as a New Year's pre ent, and for your mother to sit in and you afterwards -

you know I used the chair for a year, and if I recollect right, it is a good strong one, though plain — I am glad to hear what you wrote about your mother — Everything about fellows' old mothers is interesting to me — Give my love to Mr. and Mrs. Nash — your loving old WALT.

III

1929 *North 22nd street, Philadelphia, Wednesday, June* 20, 1877. DEAR, DEAR BOY PETE. I am stopping here now for a week or two in the house I believe I have mentioned to you before, and where I wanted you to come and see me — (and still want you if you have a chance) but I spend most of my time down at an old farm in Jersey where I have a fine secluded wood and creek and springs, where I pass my time alone, and yet not lonesome at all (often think of you, Pete, and put my arm around you and hug you up close, and give you a good buss — often).

I am still keeping pretty well for me, have improved much, indeed quite fat, and all sun burnt brick red in the face, and hands as brown as nuts — am pretty lame and paralysed yet, but walk or rather hobble sometimes half a mile and have no more (or hardly ever) of those bad, prostrated, gone in, faint spells I used to have most every day — so you see I am doing pretty well, my dear — I still make my brother's house at Camden my headquarters, and keep my room there, address my letters to Camden always.

CALAMUS

But my sister is not well, has not been for some weeks, (is soon to be confined). Upon the whole am getting along pretty well, and good spirits. The new edition of my books I sell enough of to pay my way very nicely — so I get along all right in that respect — (I don't need much) — How are they getting along at the Navy Yard? — I send them my love (I haven't forgotten the pictures, but they are a long while a-coming) — When you see Mr. Noyes tell him I should like to come on and pay him a visit this fall — And now good bye for this time, my own loving boy. Your old WALT.

IV

Kirkwood, New Jersey, Monday, July 2, 1877. DEAR BOY PETE. I still keep pretty well, and am again down here at the farm in the country, for a couple of weeks, and to stay over 4th of July. Nothing particularly new in my affairs.

As I write this (*Monday*, 10 A.M.) it is a beautiful bright breezy forenoon — and I am going now down to the creek and spring to take a bath — it is about 90 rods distant and I walk there and back. Love, love, love. Your old WALT. I still make my headquarters in Camden.

V

431 Stevens St. Camden, Sunday, Sept. 16, 4.30 P. M. [1877]. DEAR SON. I will write you a line or two any-

LETTERS OF 1876-1880

how — (it is so long since I have written anything in an envelope) — Pete, if you was to see me to-day you would almost think you saw your old Walt of six years ago — I am all fat and red and tanned.— have been down in the country most of the summer, returned the past week — feel real comfortable for me — only I am still paralyzed left side, and have pretty bad stomach troubles still at times — but thankful to God to be as well and jolly as I am. I am all alone in the house to-day, and have had a good time — fine bright warm day — been out twice for short walks, (my little dog accompanying me) — rest of the time up here alone in my 3rd story south room — done up and sent off my two books to a subscriber in England — eat my dinner alone, *wished you could be with me then, and for a couple of hours, if no more* — Pete, your papers all come regularly, and I am pleased to get them — About coming on I cannot say now, but *I shall come*, and before long — Love to Mr. and Mrs. Nash, — Love to you, my darling son, and here is a kiss for you. W. W.

VI

431 *Stevens St. cor. West, Camden, N. Jersey, Nov.* 5 [1877]. DEAR SON. I think I shall try to come on to Washington next Monday, in the noon train from here, W. Philadelphia (limited express) — Am feeling about the same — (bad enough at times — but sort o' getting used to it,) — WALT. As I understand it, the train I speak of

goes into your depot, 6th St. Must get in some ti
before dark.

VII

Camden, New Jersey, (Friday,) Dec. 20, 1878. Let
rec'd. — (And very glad every way — and thanks) —
think I am really better this winter — The cold and sn
and ice keep me in the house — else I should have be
over to the W. Phil. Depot — it would have done me go
even to have a minute and a good hold of you once me
— Nothing new in my affairs — I am doing well enou{
Tell Mr. and Mrs. N. I want to come to Wash. once mo
and I have not forgot the pictures. W. W.

VIII

2316 *Pine Street,** St. Louis, Missouri, Nov.* 5 [187·
DEAR PETE. You will be surprised to get a letter fr
me away off here — I have been taking quite a jourr
the last two months — have been out to the Roc
Mountains and Colorado (2000 miles) (Seems to me
sent you a paper six weeks ago from Denver) — I {
along very well until three weeks ago when I was tak
sick and disabled, and hauled in here in St. Louis
repairs, have been here ever since — am fixed comfc
able — still somewhat under the weather, (but have
doubt I shall be well as usual for me before long) — sl
stay here probably two or three weeks longer, and th
back east to Camden. — Pete, this is a wonderful coun

*The address of his brother Jeff, with whom he stayed in
Louis.

out here, and no one knows how big it is till he launches out in the midst of it — But there are plenty of hard-up fellows in this City and out in the mines, and all over here — you have no idea how many run ashore, get sick from exposure, poor grub, etc.— many young men, some old chaps, some boys of 15 or 16 — I met them everywhere, especially at the R. R. stoppings, out of money and trying to get home — But the general run of all these Western places, City and country is very prosperous, on the rush, plenty of people, plenty to eat, and apparently plenty of money — Colorado you know is getting to be the great silver land of the world — In Denver I visited a big smelting establishment, purifying the ore, goes through many processes — takes a week — well they showed me silver by the cart load — Then in middle Colorado, in one place, as we stopt in a mining camp, I saw rough bullion bars piled up in stacks outdoors five or six feet high, like haycocks — so it is — a few make great strikes — like the prizes in the lottery — but most are blanks — I was at Pike's Peak — I liked Denver City very much — But the most interesting part of my travel has been *the Plains*, (the great American desert the old geographies call it, but it is no desert) largely through Colorado and Western Kansas, all flat, hundreds and even thousands of miles — some real good, nearly all pretty fair soil, all for stock raising, thousands of herds of cattle, some very large — the herdsmen, (the principal common employment) a wild hardy race, always on horse

back, they call'em cow-boys altogether — I used to lik
to get among them and talk with them — I stopt som
days at a town right in the middle of those Plains, i
Kansas, on the Santa Fé road — found a soldier ther
who had known me in the war 15 years ago — wa
married and running the hotel there — I had hard wor
to get away from him — he wanted me to stay all winte
— The picture at the beginning of this letter is the S
Louis bridge over the Mississippi river — I often g
down to the river, or across this bridge — it is one of m
favorite sights — but the air of this City don't agree wit
me — I have not had a well day, (even for me) sinc
I have been here — Well, Pete, dear boy, I guess I hav
written enough — How are you getting along? I ofte
think of you and no doubt you often do of me — Go
bless you, my darling friend, and however it goes, yo
must keep up a good heart — for I do — So long — fror
your old WALT.

IX

London, Ontario, Canada, (Saturday) July 24, 188c
P. M. Am all right again for me — was sick about thre
weeks — at times pretty bad — was well taken care c
here — the best of friends both Dr. and Mrs. B. (a
human as I ever met both) — Monday morning next
start on a long Lake and St. Lawrence river trip, 90
miles, (mostly by steamer, comfortable I reckon) — gon
nearly three weeks, then back here — May write you fror
Quebec. Your papers come. W. W.

WHEN you read these I that was visible am become invisible,
Now it is you, compact, visible, realizing my poems, seeking me,
Fancying how happy you were if I could be with you and become
    your comrade;
Be it as if I were with you. (Be not too certain but I am now
    with you.)

                            Leaves of Grass (Ed'n 1892). p. 112.

LaVergne, TN USA
05 October 2009
159918LV00002B/274/P